The Amazing Animals of Iceland

A Journey Through the Country's Most Spectacular Wildlife

Copyright © 2023, Ursula Lina Velez.

All rights reserved. No part of this publication may be reproduced, distributed, or transmitted in any form or by any means, including photocopying, recording, or other electronic or mechanical methods, without the prior written permission of the publisher, except in the case of brief quotations embodied in critical reviews and certain other noncommercial uses permitted by copyright law. This book was created with the help of Artificial Intelligence technology to enhance the writing process.

The information contained in this book is for entertainment purposes only. The author and publisher of this book are not responsible for any damages or consequences arising from the use of this book's content. While every effort has been made to provide accurate and up-to-date information, readers are advised to consult with professional advisors in the relevant fields concerning any information or advice contained in this book.

All pictures used in this content are sourced from Canva and are considered license-free. Canva provides a platform that offers a variety of images that can be used for personal and commercial purposes without infringing on any copyright restrictions. The use of Canva images in this context is in compliance with Canva's terms of service and licensing agreements.

Introduction to the Animal Kingdom of Iceland 5

The Enchanting Arctic Fox: Master of Adaptation 7

The Puffin's Paradise: Breeding Grounds and Colorful Plumage 11

The Icelandic Horse: Vikings' Furry Companions 15

The Elusive Gyrfalcon: Iceland's Sky Hunter 19

Humpback Whales: Gentle Giants of the North Atlantic 23

Orca Encounters: The Dynamic Marine Mammals 27

Harlequin Ducks: The Vibrant Coastal Dwellers 31

Reindeer Royalty: Imported Monarchs of the Highlands 35

The Mystique of the Great Northern Diver 39

The White-Tailed Eagle: Iceland's Majestic Raptor 43

Atlantic Walruses: The Tusked Pinnipeds 46

The Secret Life of Grey Seals 50

Rock Ptarmigan: Masters of Camouflage 54

Icelandic Sheep: The Woolly Backbone of a Nation 58

The Charming Harbor Seal: A Coastal Delight 62

Minke Whales: The Smaller Baleen Cousins 66

The Fierce Greenland Shark: Ancient Denizens of the Deep 70

The Snow Bunting: Icy Island's Little Songbird 74

The Atlantic Salmon's Epic Journey 78

Short-eared Owls: Hunters of the Midnight Sun 82

The Atlantic Puffin's Close Relative: The Razorbill 85

The Red-throated Loon: An Arctic Coastal Gem 88

The Enigmatic Harbor Porpoise 91

Kittiwakes: The Cliffside Nesters 94

The Black Guillemot: A Contrast in Plumage 97

The Redwing: An Icelandic Songbird Saga 100

Seabird Spectacle: The Arctic Tern 103

The Unassuming Meadow Pipit 106

Eider Ducks: Guardians of the Down 109

The Wandering Whooper Swan 112

The Golden Plover: A Symbol of Spring 115

The Lesser Black-backed Gull: The Sea's Ever-Present Scavenger 118

Conclusion 121

Introduction to the Animal Kingdom of Iceland

Iceland, a land of fire and ice, is renowned for its breathtaking landscapes, thundering waterfalls, and active volcanoes. However, it is also home to a fascinating array of wildlife that has adapted to the challenging environment of this remote North Atlantic island. From the tiniest insects to the mighty whales, Iceland's animal kingdom is a testament to the resilience and adaptability of life.

The island's geographical isolation has played a significant role in shaping its unique fauna. Formed around 20 million years ago by volcanic activity, Iceland lies on the Mid-Atlantic Ridge, where the North American and Eurasian tectonic plates meet. The harsh climate and lack of land connections with other continents have restricted the number of species that have managed to colonize the island. Consequently, Iceland's native wildlife is relatively limited compared to other countries, but it is no less fascinating.

Iceland's terrestrial mammals consist primarily of the Arctic fox, the island's only native land mammal. These resourceful creatures have adapted to Iceland's unforgiving environment, changing their fur color with the seasons to blend into their surroundings. Other land mammals, such as the Icelandic horse and reindeer, were introduced by humans. The Icelandic horse, brought by the Vikings around the 9th century, is a unique breed known for its small stature, strength, and distinctive gaits. Reindeer, introduced in the 18th century, have made their home in the eastern part of the island, roaming the highlands during the summer and migrating to lower elevations in winter.

Birds are an essential part of Iceland's wildlife, with over 300 recorded species. The Atlantic puffin, with its strikingly colorful bill, is perhaps the most iconic of Iceland's birds. The island hosts a significant portion of the world's puffin population, and their breeding colonies are an important attraction for tourists and birdwatchers. The gyrfalcon, the largest falcon species, is another remarkable bird found in Iceland. Its powerful build and exceptional hunting skills make it a symbol of strength and nobility.

Other notable avian species include the white-tailed eagle, the great northern diver, the rock ptarmigan, and the snow bunting, each with their own unique characteristics and adaptations to the Icelandic environment. The island's position on the East Atlantic Flyway also makes it an important stopover for migratory birds such as the whooper swan, the red-throated loon, and various species of waders and shorebirds.

Iceland's marine life is just as captivating. Its cold, nutrient-rich waters provide an ideal habitat for a variety of marine mammals, including multiple species of whales, seals, and porpoises. Humpback whales, minke whales, and orcas are among the most commonly sighted cetaceans, while the elusive Greenland shark lurks in the deep waters surrounding the island. Seals, including the charming harbor seal and the more elusive grey seal, can often be found basking on the rocky shores or swimming in the coastal waters.

Iceland's rivers and lakes are home to a range of freshwater species, most notably the Atlantic salmon, which undertakes an epic journey from the ocean to spawn in the island's pristine rivers. Brown trout, Arctic char, and the three-spined stickleback are other noteworthy fish species found in Iceland's inland waters.

In this book, we will explore the incredible animal kingdom of Iceland, delving into the lives of the island's most fascinating creatures. Each chapter will introduce you to a different species, unveiling their unique adaptations, behavior, and ecological roles within the Icelandic ecosystem. Through this journey, you will come to appreciate the beauty and resilience of Iceland's wildlife, and the importance of preserving these extraordinary habitats for future generations to enjoy.

The Enchanting Arctic Fox: Master of Adaptation

The Arctic fox (Vulpes lagopus) holds the title of Iceland's only native land mammal, a resourceful and resilient creature that has managed to thrive in the island's harsh environment. With their stunning adaptations and ability to navigate through extreme conditions, Arctic foxes have become a symbol of strength and endurance in the face of adversity. In this chapter, we will delve into the enchanting world of the Arctic fox, exploring its unique characteristics, behaviors, and the vital role it plays in the Icelandic ecosystem.

Physical Adaptations: Camouflage and Insulation

One of the most striking features of the Arctic fox is its incredible ability to change its coat color with the seasons. This camouflage technique allows the fox to blend seamlessly into its surroundings, providing protection from predators and increasing its chances of successfully hunting prey. In the winter months, the Arctic fox sports a thick, luxurious white coat that matches the snow-covered landscape. As the snow melts and spring arrives, the fox's fur transitions to a thinner, brownish-grey coat, allowing it to blend with the rocky terrain and vegetation.

In addition to providing camouflage, the Arctic fox's fur offers exceptional insulation against the frigid Icelandic climate. Its dense underfur, combined with a layer of longer guard hairs, creates an effective barrier against the cold, enabling the fox to maintain a stable body temperature even in temperatures as low as -50°C (-58°F). This remarkable insulation also extends to the fox's paws, which are covered in thick fur to provide traction and protection against the cold while navigating icy terrain.

Resourceful Hunters and Scavengers

Arctic foxes are opportunistic feeders, with a diverse diet that reflects the availability of resources in their environment. In Iceland, they primarily feed on birds and their eggs, small mammals like voles, and carrion. During the summer months, when food is more plentiful, Arctic foxes may also consume insects, berries, and seaweed. This flexibility in their diet allows them to survive in an environment where food can be scarce.

The Arctic fox is an adept hunter, using its keen senses of smell, hearing, and sight to locate prey. In the winter months, when small mammals are hidden beneath the snow, the fox relies on its acute hearing to pinpoint their exact location. Once it has detected the prey's movements, the fox leaps high into the air and pounces, diving headfirst into the snow to capture its meal. This remarkable hunting technique, known as "mousing," enables the Arctic fox to access food resources that might otherwise be out of reach.

Social Behavior and Reproduction

Arctic foxes are primarily monogamous, forming long-term pair bonds that can last for several years. During the breeding season, which typically occurs from February to April, the male and female work together to establish a den, which can be an elaborate system of tunnels and chambers dug into the ground or snow. The female gives birth to a litter of 5 to 10 pups, sometimes even more, after a gestation period of about 52 days.

Both parents are involved in the care and upbringing of the pups, with the male providing food for the nursing female and the growing litter. The pups are born blind and helpless, relying on their mother's warmth and milk for the first few weeks of their lives. As they grow and develop, the young foxes begin to explore their surroundings and learn essential survival skills from their parents. By the time autumn arrives, the pups are fully independent and ready to face the challenges of life in the harsh Icelandic wilderness.

Conservation and Human Interaction

Arctic foxes have been hunted for their fur for centuries, leading to population declines in some areas. However, in recent years, conservation efforts have been implemented to protect these enchanting creatures and ensure their survival in the wild. In Iceland, the Arctic fox is now a protected species, with hunting only allowed under specific circumstances and within designated areas. Additionally, the establishment of nature reserves and national parks, such as Hornstrandir in the Westfjords, has provided essential habitat protection for the Arctic fox and other wildlife.

The Arctic fox also plays a vital role in the Icelandic ecosystem as a predator and scavenger. By controlling populations of small mammals and birds, the fox helps to maintain a balance within the food chain. As a scavenger, it aids in breaking down and recycling organic matter, contributing to the overall health of the ecosystem.

Climate change poses a significant threat to the Arctic fox's future, as rising temperatures and changing weather patterns can alter their habitat and food availability. In response to these challenges, researchers are closely monitoring Arctic fox populations and their behavior, working to better understand the potential impacts of climate change on this iconic species.

Coexisting with the Arctic fox

In recent years, there has been a growing interest in wildlife tourism in Iceland, with visitors flocking to the island to catch a glimpse of its unique fauna. While Arctic foxes can be elusive and are not always easy to spot, there are several locations around the island where sightings are more likely, such as the Westfjords and the highlands. For those seeking a more immersive experience, guided tours and wildlife photography workshops offer opportunities to learn more about the Arctic fox and its habitat, while contributing to local conservation efforts.

The Arctic fox's adaptability and resilience serve as a reminder of the incredible power of nature in the face of adversity. As we continue to explore the amazing animals of Iceland, we will encounter more extraordinary examples of survival and adaptation in this remarkable land. By understanding and appreciating the unique characteristics and behaviors of the Arctic fox, we can work together to protect and conserve this enchanting species for generations to come.

The Puffin's Paradise: Breeding Grounds and Colorful Plumage

The Atlantic puffin (Fratercula arctica) is undoubtedly one of Iceland's most iconic and beloved birds. With their strikingly colorful bills, black and white plumage, and endearing waddling gait, puffins have captured the hearts of locals and visitors alike. In this chapter, we will explore the enchanting world of the Atlantic puffin, delving into their breeding habits, the significance of their colorful plumage, and the crucial role they play in Iceland's coastal ecosystems.

Breeding Grounds: Coastal Colonies and Burrow Dwellers

Iceland is home to a significant portion of the world's Atlantic puffin population, with an estimated 8 to 10 million individuals breeding on the island's coastal cliffs during the summer months. Some of the most important puffin breeding colonies in Iceland include the Westman Islands, Látrabjarg cliffs in the Westfjords, and the islands of Grimsey, Lundey, and Akurey in the North.

Atlantic puffins are burrow-nesting seabirds, creating their nests in tunnels dug into the soft soil of steep coastal cliffs. These burrows can be up to 90 centimeters (35 inches) deep and provide a safe, sheltered environment for puffins to lay their eggs and rear their young. Puffins often return to the same breeding site year after year, demonstrating strong site fidelity.

During the breeding season, which typically occurs from May to August, puffins gather in large colonies known as "puffinries." These dense gatherings serve several purposes, including providing protection from predators, increasing the chances of finding a mate, and facilitating efficient communication among individuals. Puffins form monogamous pair bonds, with both males and females sharing the responsibility of incubating the single egg laid each year, as well as feeding and caring for the hatchling, called a puffling.

Colorful Plumage: Attraction and Communication

One of the Atlantic puffin's most distinctive features is its vibrant, multi-colored bill. This unique appendage is not only visually striking but also serves important functions in the puffin's social life. During the breeding season, the bill takes on its most vivid hues, with bright orange, yellow, and blue markings that make it an irresistible attraction for potential mates.

The colorful bill also plays a role in communication among puffins, with individuals using their bills to engage in various displays and behaviors. For example, puffins may perform a behavior known as "billing," in which a pair of puffins touch their bills together in a gentle, affectionate manner. This display serves to strengthen the bond between mates and establish their territory within the colony.

The puffin's black and white plumage is another notable feature that serves both an aesthetic and practical purpose. The contrasting colors provide effective camouflage, with the black upperparts blending in with the dark water when viewed from above and the white underparts helping the bird to disappear against the sky when viewed from below. This countershading helps protect puffins from predators such as large seabirds, seals, and even orcas.

A Vital Role in the Coastal Ecosystem

Puffins play a crucial role in Iceland's coastal ecosystems as predators of small fish, particularly sand eels and capelin. By consuming large quantities of these fish, puffins help regulate their populations and maintain a balance within the marine food web. In turn, puffins provide a food source for other predators, such as skuas and gulls, which may prey on puffin eggs, chicks, or even adults.

Conservation and the Future of Puffins

Although puffins are not currently considered endangered, they face several challenges that could threaten their future survival. Overfishing of key prey species, such as sand eels and capelin, can lead to food shortages for puffins, resulting in reduced breeding success and population declines. Climate change is another significant concern, as rising sea temperatures and shifting ocean currents can affect the distribution and availability of the puffins' preferred prey.

In response to these challenges, conservation efforts have been implemented to protect puffin populations and their breeding habitats. In Iceland, puffin hunting has been strictly regulated, with seasonal closures and quotas in place to ensure sustainable practices. Additionally, the establishment of marine protected areas and nature reserves helps safeguard the puffins' coastal breeding grounds, ensuring that these iconic birds have a safe place to raise their young.

Celebrating and Appreciating the Puffin's Paradise

The Atlantic puffin is an integral part of Iceland's cultural and natural heritage, symbolizing the unique and enchanting wildlife that inhabits the island's shores. Visitors to Iceland can experience the wonder of puffin colonies firsthand by embarking on guided boat tours, visiting coastal observation points, or participating in responsible wildlife photography workshops. By engaging in these activities and supporting local conservation initiatives, we can help ensure that the puffin's paradise remains a thriving part of Iceland's coastal ecosystems for generations to come.

As we continue to explore the amazing animals of Iceland, the Atlantic puffin serves as a powerful reminder of the beauty and resilience of life in this extraordinary island nation. By understanding and appreciating the puffin's unique adaptations, breeding habits, and the vital role it plays in the coastal environment, we can work together to protect and celebrate these captivating birds and the remarkable world they inhabit.

The Icelandic Horse: Vikings' Furry Companions

The Icelandic horse, a unique and cherished breed, is an essential part of Iceland's cultural heritage and national identity. Steeped in history and tradition, these small yet powerful horses have been invaluable companions to the Icelandic people for over a thousand years. In this chapter, we will explore the fascinating world of the Icelandic horse, delving into their rich history, distinctive characteristics, and the enduring bond between these remarkable animals and their human counterparts.

A Journey Through History: From Viking Steeds to Modern-Day Icons

The Icelandic horse's origins can be traced back to the ninth century when Norse settlers brought their hardy horses to the island. These early horses, bred for strength and endurance, were the foundation of the modern Icelandic breed, which has remained remarkably pure due to Iceland's isolation and strict import regulations. In fact, the Icelandic horse is one of the purest and oldest horse breeds in the world.

Throughout the centuries, Icelandic horses have played a vital role in the lives of the island's inhabitants, serving as essential means of transportation, agricultural workhorses, and beloved companions. They have been celebrated in Icelandic literature, art, and folklore, earning their place as an enduring symbol of Iceland's Viking heritage.

Distinctive Characteristics: Small Stature, Big Heart

At first glance, the Icelandic horse may seem small compared to other breeds, standing at an average height of 13 to 14 hands (52 to 56 inches). However, these compact horses are incredibly strong and muscular, with a sturdy build that belies their size. Icelandic horses are known for their thick, double-layered coats, which provide insulation against the harsh Icelandic weather, and their long, flowing manes and tails.

One of the most notable characteristics of the Icelandic horse is its unique gait repertoire. In addition to the traditional walk, trot, and canter/gallop, Icelandic horses possess two additional gaits: the tölt and the flying pace. The tölt is a smooth, four-beat gait that provides a comfortable, ground-covering ride, while the flying pace is a fast, two-beat gait used primarily for racing. These distinctive gaits set the Icelandic horse apart from other breeds and contribute to its popularity among equestrians worldwide.

A Strong Bond: The Icelandic Horse and its Human Partners

Icelandic horses are known for their friendly, curious, and intelligent nature, which has fostered a strong bond between these animals and their human partners. They are highly adaptable and versatile, excelling in various equestrian disciplines such as dressage, jumping, endurance riding, and traditional Icelandic horse competitions. The close relationship between Icelandic horses and their riders is exemplified by the many events, festivals, and competitions held annually throughout the island, where horses and riders showcase their skills and celebrate their shared heritage.

Conservation and Preservation: Safeguarding a National Treasure

The Icelandic horse population, estimated to be around 80,000 in Iceland and over 100,000 worldwide, is considered to be secure. However, the breed's genetic purity is of paramount importance to Icelanders, who have implemented strict measures to preserve this unique lineage. Importation of horses into Iceland is prohibited, and once an Icelandic horse leaves the island, it cannot return. These measures ensure that the Icelandic horse remains a distinct and cherished part of the island's cultural and genetic landscape.

Celebrating the Icelandic Horse: Tourism and Cultural Immersion

For visitors to Iceland, the opportunity to experience the Icelandic horse firsthand is a highlight of their trip. Numerous riding tours, ranging from short excursions to multi-day treks, allow visitors to explore the island's breathtaking landscapes in the company of these captivating animals. Additionally, events such as the annual Landsmót national horse competition offer a unique opportunity for both locals and tourists to witness the remarkable talents of Icelandic horses and their riders in a festive, celebratory atmosphere.

Riding an Icelandic horse is an unforgettable experience, not only because of their smooth gaits and powerful strides but also because of the deep connection between rider and horse. Riding schools and equestrian centers across the island offer lessons and training in Icelandic horsemanship, providing visitors with the chance to learn about the breed's history, unique characteristics, and traditional riding techniques.

The Icelandic horse has also captured the hearts of equine enthusiasts beyond the island's shores, with Icelandic horse associations and clubs established in numerous countries worldwide. These organizations aim to promote the breed, educate the public about Icelandic horsemanship, and foster international camaraderie among Icelandic horse enthusiasts.

The Enduring Legacy of the Icelandic Horse

As we continue to explore the amazing animals of Iceland, the Icelandic horse stands as a testament to the strength, resilience, and adaptability that define the island's unique fauna. The enduring bond between these horses and their human partners serves as a powerful reminder of the vital role that animals have played in shaping Iceland's history, culture, and identity.

By understanding and appreciating the Icelandic horse's rich heritage, distinctive characteristics, and the deep connection they share with the people of Iceland, we can work together to preserve and celebrate this remarkable breed for generations to come. In doing so, we honor not only the Icelandic horse itself but also the intrepid spirit of the Vikings who first brought these furry companions to the shores of Iceland more than a thousand years ago.

The Elusive Gyrfalcon: Iceland's Sky Hunter

The gyrfalcon (Falco rusticolus), the largest and most powerful falcon in the world, is a captivating and elusive presence in the skies of Iceland. Revered for its prowess as a hunter and its striking appearance, the gyrfalcon has long been admired by both naturalists and falconers alike. In this chapter, we will delve into the fascinating world of the gyrfalcon, exploring its distribution and habitat, hunting strategies, and the role it plays within Iceland's rich avian tapestry.

A Regal Presence: Distribution and Habitat

The gyrfalcon, native to the circumpolar regions of the Northern Hemisphere, can be found in countries such as Iceland, Greenland, Norway, Sweden, Finland, Russia, and Canada. In Iceland, the gyrfalcon is a resident species, inhabiting the island's rugged cliffs, coastal regions, and vast interior highlands. The bird's preference for remote, inaccessible areas makes it difficult to observe in the wild, contributing to its enigmatic reputation.

The gyrfalcon's habitat is characterized by its proximity to prey, which primarily consists of birds such as ptarmigans, waterfowl, and seabirds. Gyrfalcons are highly adaptable, capable of hunting in diverse environments ranging from windswept tundras to rocky coastlines. Their wide distribution and varied hunting grounds have resulted in several subspecies with distinct plumage variations, ranging from nearly pure white to dark gray.

Masters of the Sky: Hunting Strategies and Prey

As apex predators in their environment, gyrfalcons are renowned for their exceptional hunting skills. These powerful birds employ a variety of strategies to capture their prey, including stooping (diving at high speed), pursuing in level flight, and ambushing from a concealed perch. With a wingspan of up to 130 centimeters (51 inches) and a top diving speed of over 240 kilometers per hour (150 miles per hour), the gyrfalcon is a formidable predator capable of catching even the most elusive quarry.

The gyrfalcon's primary prey in Iceland is the rock ptarmigan, a well-camouflaged ground-dwelling bird that relies on its agility and speed to evade predators. Gyrfalcons also prey upon a variety of other birds, including ducks, geese, seabirds, and even other birds of prey. Their diverse diet enables them to adapt to changing food resources, ensuring their survival in Iceland's challenging and dynamic ecosystems.

A Solitary Hunter: Breeding and Social Behavior

Gyrfalcons are solitary hunters, fiercely territorial and protective of their hunting grounds. During the breeding season, which typically occurs from March to May, gyrfalcons establish nesting sites on cliff ledges or in abandoned raptor nests. Both males and females participate in the nest-building process, lining the nest with soft materials such as feathers and moss.

Once the nest is complete, the female lays a clutch of two to five eggs, which she incubates for approximately 35 days while the male provides her with food. After hatching, the chicks, known as eyases, are cared for by both parents, who feed and protect them until they fledge at around seven weeks of age. Juvenile gyrfalcons face a challenging first year, with many perishing due to harsh weather conditions, predation, or lack of food resources.

Conservation and the Future of the Gyrfalcon

The gyrfalcon is currently classified as a species of least concern on the IUCN Red List of Threatened Species. However, these majestic birds face potential threats from habitat loss, climate change, and human disturbance. In Iceland, efforts are being made to monitor gyrfalcon populations and protect their nesting sites from disturbance. Conservation initiatives such as the establishment of protected areas and the regulation of hunting activities aim to ensure the long-term survival of this magnificent species.

In addition to these conservation measures, the gyrfalcon holds a special place in the world of falconry, a centuries-old tradition that has played a crucial role in the species' preservation. Revered for their power, agility, and hunting prowess, gyrfalcons have been highly sought after by falconers for generations. This enduring interest in the gyrfalcon has contributed to a deeper understanding of the species and promoted awareness of its conservation needs.

The Gyrfalcon's Place in Iceland's Natural Heritage

As we continue to explore the amazing animals of Iceland, the elusive gyrfalcon serves as a powerful symbol of the island's rugged landscapes and the incredible diversity of life that inhabits them. The gyrfalcon's remarkable hunting abilities, striking appearance, and fascinating behavior have captured the imagination of naturalists, falconers, and wildlife enthusiasts for centuries, making it an iconic and celebrated figure in Icelandic culture and beyond.

By understanding and appreciating the gyrfalcon's unique adaptations, ecological role, and the challenges it faces in the wild, we can work together to protect and celebrate these awe-inspiring birds and the extraordinary environments they inhabit. In doing so, we ensure that the gyrfalcon's legacy as Iceland's sky hunter endures for future generations to admire and cherish.

Humpback Whales: Gentle Giants of the North Atlantic

Humpback whales (Megaptera novaeangliae), some of the most enigmatic and beloved marine mammals on Earth, grace the waters surrounding Iceland with their awe-inspiring presence. These gentle giants of the North Atlantic are renowned for their acrobatic displays, haunting songs, and the intricate social behaviors that make them a fascinating subject for scientists and whale watchers alike. In this chapter, we will delve into the captivating world of humpback whales, exploring their biology, migration patterns, and the role they play within Iceland's thriving marine ecosystems.

Biology of a Behemoth: Size, Appearance, and Adaptations

Humpback whales, members of the baleen whale family, are distinguished by their immense size, with adults reaching lengths of up to 16 meters (52 feet) and weighing as much as 40 tons. Their bodies are predominantly black or dark gray, with varying degrees of white on their undersides and flippers, which can span up to one-third of their body length. Humpback whales are easily recognized by their distinctive knobby head, covered in fleshy protuberances called tubercles, and their humped dorsal fin, from which the species derives its name.

As filter feeders, humpback whales are equipped with baleen plates in place of teeth. These plates, made of keratin, enable the whales to strain large volumes of water for small fish and krill, their primary food sources. Humpback whales are known for their innovative feeding strategies, such as bubble-net feeding, where a group of whales works together to create a "net" of bubbles around a school of fish, concentrating the prey and making it easier to consume.

The Call of the Deep: Migration and Breeding

Humpback whales undertake one of the longest migrations of any mammal, traveling thousands of kilometers between their high-latitude feeding grounds and their low-latitude breeding grounds. In the North Atlantic, humpback whales spend the summer months feeding in the productive waters around Iceland, Norway, Greenland, and eastern Canada. As winter approaches, they embark on an epic journey southward to the warmer waters of the Caribbean, where they breed and give birth.

During the breeding season, male humpback whales engage in complex courtship displays, which include acrobatic leaps, body slams, and the production of haunting, complex songs. These songs, which can last for hours, are unique to each individual and evolve over time, serving as a means of communication and competition among males.

Mothers and Calves: The Bond That Endures

Female humpback whales give birth to a single calf every two to three years, following a gestation period of approximately 11 months. Newborn calves, measuring 4 to 5 meters (13 to 16 feet) in length and weighing around 1 ton, are born in the warm, shallow waters of the breeding grounds. From the moment of birth, the bond between mother and calf is strong, with the mother providing nourishment and protection as the calf learns the essential skills needed for survival.

Humpback whale calves are weaned at around six months of age, but they often remain with their mothers for up to a year, developing a deep and enduring bond. As they grow, young humpback whales learn to navigate the challenges of their oceanic home, eventually embarking on their first long-distance migration alongside their mother.

Iceland: A Humpback Whale Haven

The waters surrounding Iceland are a vital feeding ground for humpback whales, providing an abundance of fish and krill that sustain these massive creatures throughout the summer months. The confluence of warm and cold ocean currents around Iceland creates nutrient-rich up wellings, which support thriving populations of plankton and, in turn, attract a diverse array of marine life, including humpback whales. Icelandic waters offer prime opportunities for whale watching, with several coastal towns hosting tour operators that provide visitors with unforgettable encounters with these magnificent animals.

The unique underwater topography and oceanic conditions around Iceland create a complex soundscape that can be crucial to the humpback whales' communication and navigation. Researchers in Iceland and beyond are working to better understand the intricate songs and vocalizations of humpback whales, shedding light on the complex social behaviors and communication strategies that define these enigmatic creatures.

Conservation and the Future of Humpback Whales

Though humpback whales have made a remarkable recovery since the era of commercial whaling, which decimated their populations in the 20th century, they continue to face numerous threats in the modern world. These threats include entanglement in fishing gear, ship strikes, marine pollution, climate change, and habitat degradation.

In recent years, international efforts to protect humpback whales have resulted in a dramatic increase in their population, with the species now classified as "Least Concern" on the IUCN Red List of Threatened Species. Iceland, in particular, has taken significant steps to conserve humpback whales and their habitat, enacting strict regulations on whaling, supporting research initiatives, and promoting responsible whale watching practices that minimize disturbance to the animals.

The Allure of the Humpback Whale

As we continue to explore the amazing animals of Iceland, the humpback whale stands as a powerful symbol of the island's rich marine heritage and the interconnectedness of life on our planet. These gentle giants of the North Atlantic capture our imaginations with their awe-inspiring displays, haunting songs, and the profound connections they share with one another.

By understanding and appreciating the humpback whale's unique biology, migration patterns, and the challenges they face in the wild, we can work together to protect and celebrate these extraordinary animals and the diverse ecosystems they inhabit. In doing so, we ensure that the humpback whale's legacy as a gentle giant of the North Atlantic endures for future generations to admire and cherish.

Orca Encounters: The Dynamic Marine Mammals

Orcas, or killer whales (Orcinus orca), are among the most powerful and intelligent predators on Earth, commanding a unique combination of strength, speed, and social complexity. These remarkable marine mammals, which can occasionally be seen gracing the waters around Iceland, inspire a mix of awe and fascination in those who encounter them. In this chapter, we will explore the captivating world of orcas, delving into their biology, social structure, hunting strategies, and the role they play within Iceland's diverse marine ecosystems.

A Distinctive Apex Predator: Size, Appearance, and Adaptations

Orcas are the largest members of the dolphin family, with adult males reaching lengths of up to 9 meters (30 feet) and weighing as much as 10 tons. Females, though smaller, can still reach impressive lengths of up to 7 meters (23 feet) and weigh up to 7 tons. Orcas are easily recognized by their striking black and white coloration, with a predominantly black body and white patches around the eyes, belly, and lower jaw. Their distinct dorsal fin, which can reach up to 1.8 meters (6 feet) in height in males, is another distinguishing feature.

As apex predators, orcas are well adapted for life in the ocean. They are powerful swimmers, capable of reaching speeds of up to 56 kilometers per hour (34 miles per hour), and possess a keen sense of echolocation, which enables them to navigate and locate prey in the dark depths of the ocean. Orcas have a diverse diet, preying on a wide variety of marine species, including fish, seals, sea lions, and even other whales.

A Complex Society: Pods, Family Groups, and Communication

Orcas are highly social animals, living in tight-knit family groups called pods. These pods, typically composed of a dominant female, her offspring, and other related individuals, can number anywhere from a few animals to several dozen. Each pod has its own unique dialect of vocalizations, which are used to communicate and maintain social bonds within the group.

Orcas are known for their intricate social behaviors, including cooperative hunting, play, and alloparental care, where individuals other than the mother care for and protect young calves. This complex social structure has led scientists to consider orcas as one of the few non-human animals to exhibit a form of culture, where learned behaviors are passed down through generations.

Masters of the Hunt: Strategies and Prey

Orcas are versatile hunters, employing a wide range of strategies to capture their prey. In Iceland, orcas can often be seen hunting inshore and offshore fish species, such as herring and mackerel, using coordinated group tactics to corral and disorient their quarry. Orcas are also known to target marine mammals, such as seals and porpoises, using stealth and power to overcome their prey.

One of the most remarkable hunting strategies employed by orcas is the "carousel feeding" technique, which involves a group of orcas creating waves to wash seals off ice floes, making it easier to capture them. This astonishing display of intelligence and cooperation is a testament to the orcas' ability to adapt to different prey and environments.

Iceland's Orca Encounters: Distribution and Viewing Opportunities

While orcas are not as commonly sighted in Icelandic waters as other whale species, such as humpback whales and minke whales, they can occasionally be observed along the country's coastline, particularly in areas with abundant fish populations. The best time to encounter orcas in Iceland is during the winter and spring months when they follow the migratory routes of their prey.

Several whale watching operators in Iceland offer the opportunity to observe orcas in their natural habitat, providing visitors with a rare and unforgettable experience. Responsible whale watching practices, which prioritize the well-being of the animals and minimize disturbance, are essential for ensuring that these encounters are sustainable and respectful.

Conservation and the Future of Orcas

Although orcas are not considered to be globally threatened, they face numerous challenges in today's rapidly changing world. These threats include pollution, overfishing, habitat degradation, and the increasing impacts of climate change. In some regions, orcas are also at risk due to exposure to toxic chemicals, such as PCBs, which accumulate in their blubber and can have severe health consequences.

Efforts to conserve orcas and their habitat are crucial for the long-term survival of these magnificent animals. By better understanding the orcas' biology, behavior, and the challenges they face, we can work together to develop and implement effective conservation measures that protect both the orcas and the diverse ecosystems they inhabit.

The Allure of the Orca

As we continue our exploration of Iceland's amazing animals, the orca stands as a powerful symbol of the island's rich marine heritage and the complex interplay between species in the natural world. These dynamic marine mammals captivate our imaginations with their incredible hunting prowess, elaborate social structure, and their remarkable intelligence.

By understanding and appreciating the unique qualities of orcas, their role within Iceland's marine ecosystems, and the challenges they face in the wild, we can work together to protect and celebrate these extraordinary animals and the environments they inhabit. In doing so, we ensure that the orca's legacy as a master of the ocean endures for future generations to admire and cherish.

Harlequin Ducks: The Vibrant Coastal Dwellers

Harlequin Ducks (Histrionicus histrionicus), with their distinct, vibrant plumage and unique lifestyle, are among the most striking bird species found in Iceland. These coastal dwellers, known for their preference for fast-flowing rivers and rugged seascapes, add a splash of color and intrigue to the Icelandic avifauna. In this chapter, we delve into the captivating world of Harlequin Ducks, exploring their biology, breeding habits, behavior, and the role they play within Iceland's coastal ecosystems.

A Living Mosaic: Size, Appearance, and Adaptations

Harlequin Ducks are relatively small, compact sea ducks, with males reaching lengths of 40 to 52 cm (16 to 20 inches) and females being slightly smaller. Males are particularly striking, with their dark slate-blue plumage adorned with white markings, and chestnut sides - a combination that resembles the colorful patterns of a harlequin jester, hence their name.

Females, in contrast, display a more subdued brownish plumage but are still distinctive, with three white spots on the side of the head.

As dwellers of turbulent waters, Harlequin Ducks are well adapted for life in challenging environments. Their compact bodies and strong, short wings enable them to navigate swift rivers and rough seas with remarkable agility. Additionally, their high-density plumage provides excellent insulation, allowing them to withstand the icy waters of the North Atlantic.

Seasonal Movers: Migration and Breeding

Harlequin Ducks are partial migrants, with birds breeding in freshwater habitats during the spring and summer, and moving to coastal areas for the winter months. In Iceland, they are predominantly coastal, with significant numbers breeding along the rugged coastlines and a smaller population nesting along fast-flowing rivers and streams.

Harlequin Ducks have a unique breeding strategy, with males and females forming monogamous pairs early in the winter season. Females lay their eggs in nests located close to water, typically in a protected crevice among rocks or under dense vegetation. The female assumes all the responsibility for incubating the eggs and caring for the ducklings once they hatch, while the male departs to join other males at molting sites.

Life on the Edge: Behavior and Diet

Harlequin Ducks lead an active lifestyle, spending much of their time swimming, diving, and foraging. Their diet primarily consists of aquatic invertebrates, such as crustaceans, mollusks, and insects, which they catch by diving beneath the surface. Despite their small size, Harlequin Ducks are strong and capable divers, often foraging in water several meters deep.

On land, Harlequin Ducks are less agile, moving with a characteristic waddle. However, they are excellent fliers, capable of swift, direct flight, often flying low over the water's surface.

Iceland's Harlequin Ducks: Distribution and Viewing Opportunities

In Iceland, Harlequin Ducks can be found along much of the country's coastline, as well as along certain rivers and streams. They are particularly abundant in the Westfjords and the northwestern part of the country, where the rugged, rocky coastlines offer ideal habitats. Birdwatchers and nature lovers visiting these areas during the breeding season (May to July) have a good chance of spotting these colorful ducks.

Conservation and the Future of Harlequin Ducks

While Harlequin Ducks are not globally threatened, they are susceptible to various threats, including habitat loss, pollution, and human disturbance. In Iceland, efforts are underway to monitor and protect their populations, with strict regulations in place to prevent disturbance during the breeding season.

The Allure of the Harlequin Duck

As we delve into the world of Iceland's diverse fauna, the Harlequin Duck stands as a vibrant emblem of the country's dynamic coastal ecosystems. These small yet resilient birds captivate our imaginations with their stunning plumage, unique lifestyle, and their remarkable adaptations to life in challenging environments.

Understanding and appreciating the unique qualities of Harlequin Ducks, their role within Iceland's coastal and freshwater ecosystems, and the challenges they face in the wild, can inspire us to protect and celebrate these extraordinary creatures and their habitats. In doing so, we ensure that the legacy of the Harlequin Duck as a vibrant coastal dweller endures for future generations to admire and cherish.

Reindeer Royalty: Imported Monarchs of the Highlands

Among the varied wildlife that populates Iceland, the reindeer (Rangifer tarandus) holds a unique position as the largest terrestrial mammal on the island. Introduced to the country in the 18th century, they have since adapted to the challenging Icelandic landscapes, primarily inhabiting the uninhabited highland regions. This chapter delves into the captivating world of the Icelandic reindeer, exploring their history, biology, behavior, and the role they play within Iceland's diverse ecosystems.

A Historical Journey: Introduction and Adaptation

Reindeer are not native to Iceland. They were imported from Norway in the late 18th century, intended to serve as a domesticated source of meat, hides, and antlers. However, attempts at domestication were unsuccessful, and the reindeer soon became feral. Over the years, they have adapted to their new environment, carving out a niche within the harsh, uninhabited highlands of Iceland. Today, the Icelandic reindeer population is estimated to be around 3,000 to 5,000 individuals, a testament to their resilience and adaptability.

A Majestic Presence: Size, Appearance, and Adaptations

Reindeer, also known as caribou in North America, are robust, well-adapted animals, capable of enduring the harshest of climates. Males can weigh up to 300 kg (660 lbs), while females typically weigh between 60-170 kg (130-370 lbs). One of their most distinctive features is their large antlers, which are the largest relative to body size among deer species. Both males and females grow antlers, though those of the males are significantly larger and more elaborate.

Reindeer are well adapted for life in cold, challenging environments. Their fur, a dense, two-layered coat, provides excellent insulation, while their broad, cloven hooves offer stability and traction on the icy terrain. They also have a keen sense of smell, helping them locate lichen and other food sources buried under snow.

Seasonal Migrants: Breeding and Migration

Reindeer are seasonal breeders, with a mating season, or rut, taking place in the autumn. Males compete for access to females, using their large antlers in dramatic battles of strength. Females give birth to a single calf in the spring, following a gestation period of around seven and a half months.

In Iceland, reindeer are also seasonal migrants, moving between their winter grazing lands in the lowland areas and their summer pastures in the highlands. This migration is driven by the search for food, with reindeer seeking out the tender shoots and leaves of willow and birch that emerge during the brief Icelandic summer.

A Regal Diet: Feeding Habits and Predation

Icelandic reindeer are primarily herbivores, feeding on a variety of vegetation, including grasses, sedges, leaves, and, in the winter months, lichen. Despite their large size, they have few natural predators in Iceland, with the occasional polar bear that drifts ashore on ice floes posing the only significant threat.

Iceland's Reindeer: Distribution and Viewing Opportunities

Reindeer in Iceland are primarily found in the east of the country, particularly in the highlands of East Iceland. They are most visible during the winter months when they descend to the lowlands, making this the ideal time for wildlife enthusiasts to observe and photograph them.

Conservation and the Future of Reindeer in Iceland

While reindeer are not native to Iceland, they have become an integral part of the country's fauna. Their populations are closely monitored by the Icelandic Institute of Natural History to ensure that their numbers are maintained at sustainable levels. Hunting of reindeer is regulated, with a limited number of hunting permits issued each year, primarily to control population sizes and prevent overgrazing.

Despite these measures, Icelandic reindeer face challenges, most notably from climate change. Increasingly unpredictable weather patterns and shifting vegetation zones can impact their food sources and migration patterns, potentially leading to greater competition for resources and increased vulnerability during harsh winter conditions.

The Allure of the Reindeer

As we journey through the rich tapestry of Icelandic wildlife, the reindeer stands as a symbol of resilience and adaptation. These imported monarchs of the highlands have carved out a niche for themselves in a land that is both beautiful and harsh, and in doing so, have become an integral part of Iceland's unique fauna.

Understanding the reindeer's history, their adaptations, behavior, and the role they play in Iceland's ecosystems can inspire us to appreciate these majestic creatures and their contribution to the island's biodiversity. And by recognizing the challenges they face, we can also understand the importance of conservation efforts in ensuring their continued presence in the highlands of Iceland.

The Mystique of the Great Northern Diver

The Great Northern Diver, known as the Common Loon (Gavia immer) in North America, holds a special place among the avian species of Iceland. Known for its haunting calls, striking plumage, and incredible diving skills, it's a bird that is as captivating as it is elusive. This chapter delves into the life and habits of this magnificent bird, offering a glimpse into its unique characteristics, behavior, and role within the Icelandic ecosystem.

A Stunning Spectacle: Physical Characteristics and Identification

The Great Northern Diver is a large, fish-eating bird, notable for its striking appearance. Adults can reach lengths of 70-90 cm (28-35 inches) with a wingspan of up to 152 cm (60 inches). They possess a robust body, a pointed bill, and webbed feet located far back on the body, a feature that enhances their swimming and diving capabilities but makes moving on land awkward.

In the summer, their plumage is truly a sight to behold. They sport a black head, a checkered black-and-white mantle, and a black bill. The most distinctive feature is their bright red eyes, adding an extra layer of mystique. In winter, they adopt a more muted grey-brown plumage, with the head and neck white, yet their captivating red eyes remain.

Masters of the Deep: Diet and Diving Skills

As their name suggests, Great Northern Divers are exceptional swimmers and divers. They are capable of diving to depths of up to 60 meters (200 feet) in pursuit of their prey. Their diet primarily consists of fish, but they also consume aquatic invertebrates, crustaceans, and occasionally plant material.

Their bodies are supremely adapted for life underwater. Their bones are denser than those of most birds, allowing them to submerge more easily. They also have excellent underwater vision, which, combined with their agility and speed, makes them efficient predators beneath the water surface.

Call of the Wild: Vocalizations and Breeding Habits

One of the most distinctive characteristics of the Great Northern Diver is its haunting vocalizations. These include a range of sounds from wails, yodels, to tremolos, each carrying different meanings, from signaling territory boundaries to expressing distress or alarm.

The breeding season begins in late spring, with pairs often returning to the same nesting sites year after year. The female lays one or two eggs, which both parents incubate. The young are capable of swimming and diving shortly after hatching but remain under parental care for several weeks.

A Nomadic Lifestyle: Migration and Distribution

Great Northern Divers are migratory birds. In Iceland, they are summer visitors, arriving in April and May to breed and raise their young on the country's freshwater lakes and large ponds. As autumn approaches, they migrate to spend the winter along the coastlines of the North Atlantic and Pacific, trading in their stunning summer plumage for a more muted winter attire.

The Great Northern Diver in Iceland: Viewing Opportunities and Conservation

Iceland offers excellent opportunities for viewing Great Northern Divers, particularly in the summer months when they are nesting. However, these birds are shy and easily disturbed, so it's important to observe them from a distance.

The Great Northern Diver is protected in Iceland, like all wild birds. Conservation efforts focus on preserving their breeding habitats and monitoring their populations. Despite facing challenges from habitat loss and environmental pollution, their numbers in Iceland remain stable, ensuring their enchanting calls continue to echo across the country's tranquil lakes.

In Conclusion: The Enigma of the Great Northern Diver

Our exploration of the Icelandic animal kingdom brings us face to face with a host of fascinating creatures, each with their unique stories and roles within the island's ecosystems. The Great Northern Diver is no exception, adding its unique melody to Iceland's symphony of wildlife.

These birds, with their captivating red eyes and haunting calls, embody the mystique and allure of the Icelandic wilderness. They remind us of the diversity and complexity of life that thrives in this land of fire and ice. Their resilience, adaptability, and sheer beauty symbolize the untamed spirit of Iceland's natural world.

Despite their elusive nature, the presence of the Great Northern Divers in the tranquil Icelandic landscapes leaves an indelible impression on those fortunate enough to witness them. They stand as a symbol of the country's rich biodiversity and the importance of conserving these unique habitats for future generations to explore and appreciate.

The White-Tailed Eagle: Iceland's Majestic Raptor

The saga of Iceland's wildlife would be incomplete without the mention of its largest bird of prey, the White-tailed Eagle (Haliaeetus albicilla). This majestic bird, with its impressive size, distinctive appearance, and soaring flight, is a symbol of freedom and strength. This chapter explores the fascinating world of the White-tailed Eagle, shedding light on its characteristics, habits, and the vital role it plays in the Icelandic ecosystem.

Awe-Inspiring Appearance: Identifying the White-tailed Eagle

The White-tailed Eagle is a large raptor, and it's impossible to mistake it for any other bird when seen in all its glory. An adult can reach lengths of 66-94 cm (26-37 inches) with an impressive wingspan that can range from 1.78 to 2.45 meters (5.8 to 8.0 feet). The bird is aptly named for its wedge-shaped white tail, which contrasts sharply with its dark brown body. It has a pale, hooked beak, and its eyes, bright and piercing, are a vivid yellow.

A Predator's Palette: Diet and Hunting

White-tailed Eagles are carnivores and opportunistic feeders. Their diet primarily consists of fish and birds, but they have been known to take small mammals and carrion when available. Their hunting strategy often involves soaring high and then swooping down to snatch prey with their strong, sharp talons. However, they're also known to scavenge, especially in the harsh Icelandic winters when live prey is scarce.

Breeding and Nesting: A Lifelong Bond

White-tailed Eagles are monogamous and form lifelong pairs. Their nests, called eyries, are built high in cliffs or trees and are reused and added to each year, becoming massive structures over time. Breeding season in Iceland starts in April, with females typically laying one to three eggs. Both parents share incubation duties and, once hatched, the eaglets remain in the nest for around ten to twelve weeks.

A Rarity Reclaimed: Population and Conservation

The White-tailed Eagle, once common in Iceland, faced near extinction in the early 20th century due to hunting, poisoning, and habitat destruction. However, thanks to extensive conservation efforts, the population has been gradually recovering. Today, they are a protected species in Iceland, and their population, though small, is stable and increasing.

Despite the successful conservation measures, White-tailed Eagles still face threats, including habitat disturbance and secondary poisoning from eating poisoned prey. Continued conservation work is essential to ensure the survival of this magnificent bird in the wild landscapes of Iceland.

The White-Tailed Eagle in Icelandic Culture

The White-tailed Eagle holds a special place in Icelandic culture and folklore. Its strength and majestic appearance have earned it respect and admiration, and it often features in

Icelandic sagas and folklore as a symbol of power and freedom.

Final Thoughts: The Splendor of the White-Tailed Eagle

As we delve into the stories of Iceland's remarkable wildlife, the White-tailed Eagle stands as a testament to nature's resilience and the power of conservation. It is a living symbol of the wilderness, embodying the raw, untamed beauty that makes Iceland's fauna so unique.

Witnessing a White-tailed Eagle in flight, with its broad wings outstretched against the backdrop of Iceland's dramatic landscapes, is an unforgettable experience. It serves as a reminder of the wonders that exist in the natural world and our responsibility to protect and preserve them.

Atlantic Walruses: The Tusked Pinnipeds

In this chapter, we turn our attention to the frigid waters surrounding Iceland, where we encounter a species that encapsulates the hardy resilience of the country's fauna: the Atlantic Walrus (Odobenus rosmarus rosmarus). These robust and fascinating marine mammals, easily identifiable by their large tusks and whiskered faces, are among the most compelling species found in the North Atlantic region.

Distinguishing Features: Unmistakable Appearance

The Atlantic Walrus is a marine mammal belonging to the pinniped family, which includes seals and sea lions. They are notably recognized for their long, prominent tusks, which can reach up to a meter in length in males. These tusks are actually enlarged canine teeth and are found in both males and females, although they are generally larger and more robust in males.

Their skin is thick and wrinkled, providing insulation against the cold Arctic waters, and they possess a layer of blubber that can be up to 15 cm thick. A walrus's color varies with the temperature: in the cold, they appear pale and almost white, while in warmer conditions, they can be nearly reddish-brown.

Their physical uniqueness extends to their size, with males reaching up to 3.6 meters in length and weighing up to 1,500 kilograms, while females are slightly smaller.

Marine Adaptations: Life in the Cold Waters

Walruses are well-adapted to life in the frigid North Atlantic. Their layer of blubber not only provides insulation but also acts as an energy reserve. The vibrissae, or whiskers, on their snouts are highly sensitive, helping them detect shellfish, their main food source, on the ocean floor.

Their tusks serve multiple purposes: they aid in hauling their hefty bodies out of the water onto ice floes, are used in battles for dominance, and help in foraging for food under the sea ice.

Social Creatures: Walrus Behavior

Walruses are very social and are usually found in large, tightly packed groups. They communicate with a variety of vocalizations, claps, and bellows, and physical contact is common. During the breeding season, males, known as bulls, become particularly vocal, using complex calls to attract females and intimidate rivals.

Females, or cows, give birth to a single calf after a gestation period of about 15 months. The bond between a cow and her calf is strong, and the young walrus may stay with its mother for up to two years.

Walruses and Iceland: An Unusual Sight

While walruses are not typically thought of as Icelandic animals, historical accounts and archaeological evidence suggest that they were once more prevalent around the island. Today, sightings in Iceland are rare and often involve young, vagrant individuals who have strayed from their usual range.

However, each sighting sparks interest and reminds us of the diverse array of marine life that the waters surrounding Iceland support. These occasional visitors are a testament to the richness of the North Atlantic and its role as a crucial habitat for an array of marine species.

The Atlantic Walrus: A Symbol of Arctic Life

Atlantic Walruses, with their distinctive tusks and whiskered faces, are emblematic of the Arctic's unique biodiversity. They are a testament to the adaptability and resilience of life in some of the harshest conditions on the planet.

Their presence, even if infrequent, adds another layer to the rich tapestry of Icelandic wildlife. Each sighting of a walrus along Iceland's shores serves as a reminder of the island's historical and ecological connections to these fascinating marine mammals.

As we delve further into the animal kingdom of Iceland, we continue to unearth unique stories of survival, adaptation, and diversity. The Atlantic Walrus, with its unmistakable tusks and jovial disposition, serves as an ambassador for the extraordinary creatures that call the icy waters of the North Atlantic home.

The Atlantic Walrus also presents a remarkable example of the interconnectedness of life within the Arctic Circle. Their diet, largely composed of shellfish, impacts the ocean floor ecosystem, proving that even the smallest creatures play a critical role in the life cycle of one of the Arctic's most distinctive inhabitants.

Moreover, their social nature and complex behaviors offer intriguing insights into the social dynamics of marine mammals. The tightly-knit herds, the vocal and physical communication, and the strong mother-calf bonds - all these aspects emphasize the intricate social structures and relationships that exist within walrus communities.

Yet, the Atlantic Walrus is not without its challenges. Climate change, hunting, and human disturbance pose significant threats to their populations. Their dependence on sea ice for resting and giving birth makes them particularly vulnerable to global warming. As the ice recedes, they are forced to swim longer distances in search of food, leading to increased stress and mortality, especially among calves.

Conservation efforts are underway to protect and preserve these iconic creatures. As part of the global community, it's our collective responsibility to support these efforts, ensuring that future generations also get a chance to be captivated by the charm of the tusked pinnipeds.

As we conclude our journey with the Atlantic Walrus, we are reminded of the diversity, adaptability, and resilience of the fauna that graces the land and seas of Iceland. From the mountain peaks to the ocean depths, each creature, large or small, has a tale to tell, a role to play, and a lesson to impart.

The Secret Life of Grey Seals

Our next encounter in the incredible world of Icelandic wildlife introduces us to a marine species known for its playful behavior and soulful eyes: the Grey Seal (Halichoerus grypus). Also known as the Atlantic Grey Seal, this charismatic creature leads a fascinating life that is closely intertwined with the rich marine ecosystems surrounding Iceland.

Characteristics: Identifying the Grey Seal

Grey Seals are one of the largest seal species in the world. They have a distinctive elongated, horse-like head, which is the source of their scientific name, Halichoerus grypus, meaning "hook-nosed sea pig." Males, or bulls, are larger than females, or cows, with bulls reaching up to 3 meters in length and weighing between 170 and 310 kilograms. Cows are smaller, usually measuring around 2 meters and weighing between 100 and 190 kilograms.

Grey Seals' fur varies in color from grey to brown, with unique patterns of spots that are darker in females and lighter in males. Their large, expressive eyes are adapted for underwater vision, while their powerful flippers enable them to be agile swimmers.

Habitat and Diet: An Aquatic Lifestyle

Grey Seals inhabit the cold, nutrient-rich waters of the North Atlantic. In Iceland, they are commonly found along the country's rocky coastlines and offshore islands, where they haul out onto the land for resting, molting, and breeding.

As opportunistic feeders, Grey Seals have a varied diet that mainly includes fish, such as cod, herring, and flatfish, as well as squid and octopus. Their excellent underwater vision and sensitive whiskers help them locate prey in the often murky depths of the North Atlantic.

Social Structure and Reproduction: Community Life

Grey Seals are generally less social than some other seal species, but they still form groups, especially during the breeding season. Bulls establish territories in breeding colonies, or rookeries, where they compete for access to receptive females.

Females give birth to a single pup each year, usually between September and November. At birth, pups are covered in a dense, white fur known as lanugo. Mothers are devoted caregivers, nursing their pups with rich, fatty milk for about three weeks, during which the pup can triple its weight. During this period, the mother fasts and can lose up to a third of her body weight.

The Grey Seal in Iceland: A Common Sight

Grey Seals are one of the most common marine mammals seen in Iceland. They are often spotted lounging on rocky shores or bobbing in the water near the coast. Their curious and inquisitive nature often leads them to approach boats, offering observers memorable, up-close encounters.

However, like other marine species, Grey Seals face threats from human activities, such as fishing net entanglements and marine pollution. They are also vulnerable to changes in food availability due to overfishing and climate change.

Yet, despite these challenges, Grey Seals continue to thrive in Iceland's waters, adding a touch of charm and intrigue to the country's diverse marine landscapes.

Unveiling the Secrets of the Grey Seal

The Grey Seal's adaptability, fascinating social structure, and endearing behavior captivate our attention and deepen our appreciation for the diverse array of life that calls Iceland home. As we observe these seals, whether they're playfully riding the waves, lounging on rocky outcrops, or tenderly caring for their pups, we're reminded of the strength and resilience of Iceland's wildlife.

From their unique morphology to their complex breeding behavior, every facet of the Grey Seal's life is a testament to nature's ability to adapt and flourish, even in challenging conditions. They remind us of the intricate interactions and dependencies that tie every species within an ecosystem together. Their continued survival hinges not just on the health of the ocean they live in, but also on the abundance and diversity of their prey, the safety of their breeding grounds, and the stability of their environment.

Grey Seals also hold an important role in Iceland's cultural history, featuring in many local legends and folklore. For centuries, these creatures have sparked the curiosity and imagination of the Icelandic people, often being associated with mythical beings or spirits. Today, they continue to be a beloved part of Iceland's natural heritage, and efforts are being made to ensure their survival for future generations to appreciate and learn from.

Under the watchful eye of conservationists, researchers continue to study the Grey Seals of Iceland, hoping to uncover more about their life history, population dynamics, and the challenges they face. These studies are not only critical for the conservation of the Grey Seal, but they also provide valuable insights into the health of the marine ecosystems they inhabit.

Protecting the Grey Seal and its habitat is a task that extends beyond the boundaries of science. It's a shared responsibility that involves governments, communities, and individuals alike. By mitigating the impacts of human activities, enforcing sustainable fishing practices, and reducing marine pollution, we can all contribute to the conservation of the Grey Seal and the preservation of Iceland's rich biodiversity.

As we wrap up our exploration of the secret life of the Grey Seal, we are left with a renewed sense of wonder and admiration for the intricate tapestry of life that thrives in and around the shores of Iceland. The Grey Seal serves as a powerful symbol of the resilience and beauty of Iceland's wildlife, inviting us to pause, observe, and appreciate the miracles of nature that surround us.

Rock Ptarmigan: Masters of Camouflage

Our exploration of the diverse fauna of Iceland takes us from the ocean depths to the rugged highlands, where we encounter a bird species that embodies the spirit of survival and adaptation. Meet the Rock Ptarmigan (Lagopus muta), a remarkable creature known for its extraordinary ability to blend into its surroundings. Its mastery of camouflage, coupled with its hardy nature, allows it to thrive in the harsh, subarctic landscapes of Iceland.

Physical Features: The Bird of Many Coats

The Rock Ptarmigan is a medium-sized bird, roughly the size of a chicken. One of its most striking features is its seasonal change in plumage, a fascinating adaptation to the extreme climatic variations of its habitat. In summer, the bird sports a mottled brown coat, perfectly matching the rocky terrain. As winter approaches, the Rock Ptarmigan undergoes a complete transformation, shedding its summer coat for a pure white one, offering seamless camouflage against the snow-covered landscapes.

These birds have sturdy legs covered in feathers, which not only provide warmth in the biting cold but also act as 'snowshoes' to help them walk on soft snow. The male, or cock, has a prominent red eyebrow, or comb, which becomes more pronounced during the breeding season.

Habitat and Diet: Surviving the Highlands

Inhabiting the rocky slopes and heather moorlands of Iceland, Rock Ptarmigans are primarily ground dwellers, although they can fly short distances when threatened. Their preferred habitat consists of areas with abundant vegetation and nearby rocks or shrubs for cover.

Rock Ptarmigans are omnivorous, with a diet that changes according to the season. In summer, they consume a variety of insects, leaves, flowers, and berries. Come winter, they switch to a diet mainly consisting of buds, twigs, and seeds of birch and willow.

Breeding and Behavior: The Cycle of Life

The breeding season for Rock Ptarmigans begins in late April or early May. Males establish territories and compete for females through displays of dominance, including spreading their tail feathers and flashing their red eyebrows.

Females lay a clutch of 6-10 eggs in a ground nest lined with plant material and feathers. The female incubates the eggs for about three weeks, while the male stands guard nearby. Upon hatching, the chicks are precocial, meaning they are relatively mature and mobile, able to forage for food with guidance from their mother.

Rock Ptarmigan in Icelandic Culture: A Symbol of Resilience

The Rock Ptarmigan holds a special place in Icelandic culture. It is an important game bird and was traditionally hunted for food, particularly around Christmas time. However, due to fluctuations in population numbers in recent years, hunting restrictions have been implemented to ensure the sustainability of the species.

The Ptarmigan's ability to survive and thrive in the harsh Icelandic environment has led to it being regarded as a symbol of resilience and perseverance. This respect for the Ptarmigan is reflected in local folklore and literature, where the bird often features as a character embodying strength and survival.

Conservation Status: Adapting to Change

While the Rock Ptarmigan is not currently considered a threatened species, it faces challenges from habitat alteration due to climate change and human activities. Changes in vegetation patterns, driven by global warming, could impact their food sources and breeding sites.

Understanding the Rock Ptarmigan

As we delve into the life of the Rock Ptarmigan, we uncover tales of survival, adaptation, and resilience that echo across the highlands of Iceland. These birds are not merely inhabitants of these landscapes but are active participants in the ecological processes that shape them.

Their cyclical molt, changing with the seasons, reminds us of the intricate links between organisms and their environments, a dynamic dance of change and adaptation. By blending so seamlessly into their surroundings, Rock Ptarmigans teach us about the profound connections that bind every creature to its habitat.

Through its diet, the Rock Ptarmigan helps in seed dispersal, contributing to the growth and spread of vegetation across the highlands. This, in turn, influences the entire ecosystem, affecting everything from the distribution of other animal species to the stability of the soil.

The Rock Ptarmigan's breeding cycle provides another window into the rhythms of nature. From the competitive displays of males to the dedicated incubation of eggs by females, and the rapid growth and development of chicks, each stage presents a captivating display of natural behavior driven by the primal urge to survive and reproduce.

From a conservation perspective, the Rock Ptarmigan serves as an important indicator species. Fluctuations in its population can reflect changes in the environment, providing crucial insights into broader ecological shifts. Their sensitivity to habitat change makes them a valuable sentinel in our efforts to monitor the impacts of climate change.

Yet, understanding the Rock Ptarmigan extends beyond just its ecological role. This bird holds a symbolic resonance in Icelandic culture, embodying values of resilience and perseverance that resonate with the people's own experiences of living in this challenging environment.

In the face of hunting pressures and environmental changes, the Rock Ptarmigan's continued survival is a testament to its incredible adaptability. As we move forward, it is our shared responsibility to ensure that this remarkable bird continues to thrive, preserving not only a key component of Iceland's biodiversity but also a significant part of its cultural heritage.

As we conclude our exploration of the Rock Ptarmigan, we are left with a profound sense of wonder and respect for these masters of camouflage. Their story is a powerful reminder of the resilience of life in even the harshest conditions. They stand as a testament to the beauty and complexity of the natural world, and of our crucial role in safeguarding it for generations to come.

Icelandic Sheep: The Woolly Backbone of a Nation

As we continue our journey through the fascinating world of Icelandic fauna, we encounter a creature that, in many ways, has been instrumental in shaping the culture and economy of the nation. The Icelandic Sheep, an unassuming yet hardy animal, has been an integral part of Icelandic life for over a millennium. This chapter delves into the world of these woolly wonders, exploring their unique characteristics, their role in Icelandic society, and the challenges they face in a rapidly changing world.

A Breed Apart: Understanding the Icelandic Sheep

The Icelandic Sheep, a breed unto itself, is a direct descendant of the Northern European short-tailed sheep brought to the island by the first Viking settlers in the late ninth century. Over the centuries, this breed has adapted to the harsh Icelandic environment, becoming a distinct and uniquely adapted species.

Physically, Icelandic Sheep are medium-sized with both sexes bearing horns. They possess a dual coat consisting of the outer 'togi' and the inner 'þel'. The 'togi' is long, tough, and water-resistant, protecting the sheep from harsh weather, while the 'þel' is soft, insulating, and used for finer woolen goods.

Icelandic Sheep are known for their excellent foraging capabilities. During the harsh winter months, they can dig through the snow to reach the vegetation beneath, a trait that has allowed them to thrive in an environment where other breeds might struggle.

More Than Wool: The Role of Icelandic Sheep

The role of Icelandic Sheep extends beyond their wool production. They have been integral to Iceland's agricultural economy since the time of the Viking settlers. Their meat is a staple of the Icelandic diet, with traditional dishes such as 'Hangikjöt' (smoked lamb), 'Svið' (sing-singed sheep's head), and 'Slátur' (a type of haggis), still popular today.

Icelandic Sheep are also prized for their milk, which is used to produce cheese and Skyr, a traditional Icelandic dairy product similar to yogurt. Even their horns have been utilized, traditionally crafted into various tools and ornaments.

In addition, Icelandic Sheep have played a significant ecological role. Over centuries, their grazing has shaped the vegetation and landscapes of Iceland, influencing everything from plant diversity to soil stability.

The Annual Round-Up: A Time-Honored Tradition

One of the most enduring traditions associated with Icelandic Sheep is the annual round-up, or 'Réttir'. Each autumn, farmers and townsfolk alike take to the hills on foot or horseback to round up the sheep from their summer grazing grounds in the highlands.

This communal event, often involving entire communities, is followed by a sorting process where sheep are returned to their rightful owners based on earmarkings. 'Réttir' is more than just a farming necessity; it is a social event, often accompanied by singing, dancing, and feasting, reflecting the deep-rooted connection between the people of Iceland and their sheep.

Threats and Challenges: The Future of Icelandic Sheep

Like many other species worldwide, Icelandic Sheep face challenges from climate change. Changes in vegetation, unpredictable weather patterns, and increased risk of disease are potential threats. Despite their hardiness, these shifts in their environment could have significant impacts on their survival and well-being.

Further, modernization and changes in agricultural practices could also pose challenges. As Iceland becomes more urbanized, and as younger generations move away from farming, the future of this traditional way of life comes into question.

Conclusion: Celebrating the Woolly Backbone of a Nation

The story of Icelandic Sheep is not just a tale of survival and adaptation; it is a testament to the profound connections between humans and the animals they depend upon. These woolly creatures have shaped the cultural, economic, and ecological landscape of Iceland, intertwining their lives with the people who inhabit this striking land.

The Icelandic Sheep's contributions extend far beyond the physical. They have inspired folk tales, influenced art, and even shaped the Icelandic language, with more than 100 terms related to sheep and wool. Their influence permeates Icelandic literature, from medieval sagas to modern narratives, echoing the enduring significance of these animals.

Icelandic Sheep are also integral to sustainable farming practices in Iceland. Their ability to graze on rough terrains reduces the need for mechanized farming methods, thus limiting soil erosion, a significant environmental concern in Iceland. As climate change continues to challenge traditional farming practices, the adaptability and resilience of Icelandic Sheep may become even more critical.

Despite the challenges they face, the Icelandic Sheep's future is far from bleak. Conservation efforts are underway to preserve this unique breed and its genetic diversity. These initiatives are backed by an understanding of the sheep's ecological and cultural significance, and a desire to protect and promote sustainable farming practices.

The modern Icelandic ethos, deeply rooted in respect for nature and sustainability, bodes well for these initiatives. There is also a renewed interest in traditional practices, including sheep farming and wool production, particularly among younger generations.

As we conclude our exploration of the Icelandic Sheep, we appreciate the lessons these humble creatures offer. They remind us of the enduring power of adaptation, the value of sustainability, and the profound connections between humans and the natural world. The Icelandic Sheep are indeed the woolly backbone of their nation, supporting not just an industry, but a way of life.

The Charming Harbor Seal: A Coastal Delight

As we continue our journey into the fascinating world of Icelandic animals, we turn our attention to the delightful creature that graces the coastlines of the country – the Harbor Seal. From its playful nature to its unique adaptations, the Harbor Seal offers a charming spectacle that adds color to the coastal fauna of Iceland. This chapter explores the intriguing world of these coastal delights, their role in the marine ecosystem, and the challenges they face in the contemporary world.

Introduction: A Glimpse into the World of the Harbor Seal

Harbor Seals, scientifically known as Phoca vitulina, are one of the most common marine mammals found along Iceland's extensive coastline. They are one of the two seal species that breed in Iceland, the other being the Grey Seal. The Harbor Seal, however, is smaller and more widespread, making them a more familiar sight to locals and tourists alike.

Harbor Seals in Iceland are known for their distinctive spotted coats, varying from silver or gray to brown or black. Their bodies are streamlined for efficient swimming, with a round head, robust body, and flippers that propel them through the water with remarkable agility.

A Coastal Lifestyle: Adapting to the Marine Environment

Harbor Seals are well-adapted to their marine environment. They have a layer of blubber for insulation against the cold Icelandic waters and can slow down their heart rate to conserve oxygen during deep dives. These seals are also equipped with excellent vision and hearing, which help them navigate and hunt efficiently underwater.

The diet of Harbor Seals consists mainly of fish, such as cod, herring, and sand eels, but they also consume squid and crustaceans. Their hunting strategy is a testament to their adaptability, altering their diet based on the availability of prey.

Harbor Seals are semi-aquatic, spending significant amounts of time on land, especially during the breeding season. They favor sandy or rocky coastlines, islands, and skerries, where they haul out to rest, molt, give birth, and nurse their pups.

The Pupping Season: A Time of Growth and Vulnerability

The pupping season, which occurs from June to July in Iceland, is a special time in the life cycle of Harbor Seals. Females give birth to a single pup, which they nurse with high-fat milk for about four to six weeks. The pups are born well-developed, capable of swimming and diving within hours of birth, a crucial adaptation for survival in the challenging marine environment.

However, the pupping season is also a period of vulnerability for Harbor Seals. Pups can get separated from their mothers due to disturbances or strong tides. Additionally, they are susceptible to predation and diseases, especially in areas where they congregate in large numbers.

Harbor Seals and Humans: A Complex Relationship

Harbor Seals have a complex relationship with humans. On one hand, they are a tourist attraction, drawing wildlife enthusiasts who delight in watching their playful antics. They also play an important role in the marine ecosystem, contributing to the balance of species in their coastal habitats.

On the other hand, Harbor Seals are sometimes seen as competitors by fishermen, as they can become entangled in fishing nets or deplete fish stocks. In the past, this has led to conflict and even culls. However, in recent years, efforts have been made to better understand and manage these interactions to protect both the seals and the interests of local communities.

Threats and Conservation: Safeguarding the Future of Harbor Seals

Like many marine species, Harbor Seals face a range of threats. These include pollution, overfishing, habitat loss, climate change, and human disturbances. In particular, marine pollution, such as plastic waste and toxins, can have severe impacts on seal health, affecting their immune system and reproductive capacity. Overfishing can deplete their food resources, while habitat loss due to coastal development can limit their haul-out and breeding sites.

Climate change presents a more complex challenge. Rising sea levels can submerge haul-out sites, while warming ocean temperatures can disrupt fish populations and hence the seals' food supply. Changing ice conditions may also affect the distribution and behavior of seals, although the implications of this for Harbor Seals in Iceland are not yet fully understood.

Human disturbances, particularly during the sensitive pupping season, can cause stress and disruption to Harbor Seals. Uncontrolled tourism, recreational activities, and boat traffic can lead to seals being flushed into the water, wasting energy and potentially separating mothers from their pups.

However, the story is not all bleak. Recognizing the threats facing Harbor Seals, conservation measures have been implemented to protect them. These include legal protection against hunting, the establishment of protected areas, and guidelines to minimize human disturbance. Research is also being conducted to monitor seal populations and understand their ecology and behavior better.

Public awareness and education programs are crucial components of these conservation efforts. By fostering a greater understanding and appreciation of Harbor Seals, these programs aim to promote responsible behavior among locals and tourists alike, ensuring that people can enjoy watching these charming animals without causing them harm.

Conclusion: The Harbor Seal - A Symbol of the Icelandic Coast

In conclusion, the Harbor Seal is a charming and essential part of Iceland's coastal ecosystems. While they face numerous challenges, efforts are underway to ensure their survival. As we watch a Harbor Seal bobbing in the waves or basking on a rocky shore, we are reminded of the rich biodiversity of Iceland and the responsibility we all share in safeguarding it. Through understanding, respect, and care, we can ensure that future generations will continue to delight in the sight of these coastal dwellers.

As we move on to the next chapters, we will delve into the lives of other fascinating Icelandic animals, each with their own tales of adaptation, survival, and coexistence with humans in this remarkable land. Whether they roam the highlands, soar the skies, or grace the coasts and seas, these animals collectively weave the tapestry of life that makes Iceland's nature so compelling and unique.

Minke Whales: The Smaller Baleen Cousins

As we delve deeper into the marine life of Iceland, we encounter the Minke Whale, a creature of fascinating behaviors and adaptations. It is one of the smallest baleen whales, yet its presence in the North Atlantic waters surrounding Iceland is anything but insignificant. This chapter will guide you through the life of the Minke Whale, its ecological role, and the conservation issues it faces in the modern world.

Introduction: Unveiling the Minke Whale

The Minke Whale (Balaenoptera acutorostrata) belongs to the rorqual family, which includes the largest animal ever to have lived – the Blue Whale. However, Minke Whales are the smallest member of this family, with adults measuring around 7-10 meters in length. They are characterized by a sleek, dark-grey body, a pointed rostrum, and a white band on each flipper, which can be a striking sight against the deep blue backdrop of the ocean.

An Oceanic Existence: Adaptations and Behaviors

Minke Whales are well-adapted for their oceanic existence. Their streamlined bodies allow them to swim at speeds of up to 20 km/h, and they can dive for up to 20 minutes to hunt for food. Their diet primarily consists of krill and small schooling fish such as herring and capelin, which they gulp in large quantities using their baleen plates to filter feed.

Notably, Minke Whales are solitary creatures, typically seen alone or in small groups of two or three. They have a unique 'breaching' behavior, where they leap out of the water and splash back down – a spectacle that can be thrilling to observe.

Reproduction and Life Cycle: From Calves to Adults

The reproductive cycle of the Minke Whale is a testament to the resilience of life in the harsh marine environment. Females give birth to a single calf every two years following a gestation period of around ten months. The calves are born in warmer waters during winter and are nursed for about five months. Upon reaching sexual maturity at 6-8 years, females embark on the same nurturing path, continuing the circle of life.

Minke Whales and Humans: A Relationship Marked by Wonder and Conflict

The relationship between humans and Minke Whales has been complex, marked by both wonder and conflict. For centuries, these creatures have captivated the human imagination, their breaching and surfacing behaviors providing a thrilling spectacle for sailors and, more recently, whale-watchers.

However, Minke Whales have also been the target of commercial whaling due to their relative abundance. Although international regulations have greatly reduced whaling activities, some countries, including Iceland, have continued to hunt Minke Whales, raising concerns about sustainability and animal welfare.

Conservation Efforts and Challenges: Towards a Sustainable Coexistence

In response to the threats facing Minke Whales, several conservation efforts have been put in place. Internationally, the International Whaling Commission regulates whaling activities and sets quotas to prevent over-exploitation. Nationally, Iceland has established several marine protected areas where whaling is prohibited, providing safe havens for these creatures.

However, challenges remain. Climate change threatens to disrupt the marine ecosystems upon which Minke Whales depend. Warmer ocean temperatures may affect the distribution and abundance of krill, the primary food source for Minke Whales. Moreover, noise pollution from shipping and offshore drilling can disrupt whale communication and navigation, leading to stress and even strandings.

Conclusion: Appreciating the Minke Whale

Despite their smaller size compared to their baleen relatives, Minke Whales play a crucial role in the marine ecosystems of Iceland. They are a key predator in the food chain, helping to maintain balance in the oceanic ecosystem. Their presence also supports Iceland's whale-watching industry, contributing to the local economy and promoting a greater appreciation for marine wildlife.

Yet, the survival of Minke Whales is intricately linked with the health of our oceans. Their struggles reflect broader issues facing marine ecosystems, from over-exploitation to climate change. As we reflect on the life of the Minke Whale, we are reminded of our shared responsibility in safeguarding the world's oceans and their inhabitants.

Looking forward, conservation strategies must continue to evolve, taking into account the changing conditions of our oceans and the unique biology and behavior of Minke Whales. Research plays a crucial role in this endeavor, helping us to better understand these creatures and to develop more effective conservation strategies. Technologies such as satellite tagging and DNA analysis are providing new insights into the lives of Minke Whales, from their migration patterns to their feeding behaviors.

Public awareness and education are equally important. By fostering a greater understanding and appreciation of Minke Whales, we can inspire individuals and communities to take action in their conservation. Whether it's making sustainable seafood choices, reducing plastic waste, or supporting marine protected areas, each of us can contribute to the survival of Minke Whales.

The Fierce Greenland Shark: Ancient Denizens of the Deep

In this chapter, we journey into the frigid depths of the North Atlantic and Arctic oceans surrounding Iceland, into the domain of one of the oldest and most mysterious creatures on the planet – the Greenland Shark. Known for its longevity, unique adaptations, and the fascinating role it plays in the marine ecosystem, the Greenland Shark is a marvel of evolution.

Unveiling the Greenland Shark: A Primer

The Greenland Shark (Somniosus microcephalus) is a large, slow-moving creature, often reaching lengths of up to 5 meters, though specimens as long as 7 meters have been reported. With a robust, cylindrical body and a short, rounded snout, the Greenland Shark's appearance is as intriguing as its lifestyle. Its skin ranges from shades of gray to brown, providing the perfect camouflage against the ocean's dark depths.

A Life in the Depths: Adaptations and Survival

Living in the icy, deep waters of the Arctic and North Atlantic, the Greenland Shark has evolved a suite of adaptations that allow it to thrive in these harsh conditions. The shark is capable of living in depths ranging from the surface to over 2,200 meters, with the ability to withstand the crushing pressures and low temperatures of the deep sea.

One of the most remarkable traits of the Greenland Shark is its incredible longevity. Recent research suggests that these sharks can live for at least 272 years, and possibly up to 500 years, making them the longest-lived vertebrates known on Earth. This slow growth rate and long lifespan are likely adaptations to the cold, nutrient-poor environment in which they live.

Feeding Behavior: Scavengers of the Sea

The Greenland Shark is an opportunistic feeder, consuming a wide variety of prey. Its diet is known to include fish, squid, and smaller sharks, and even marine mammals such as seals. The shark's slow speed might suggest it's an ineffective predator, but its ability to hunt in total darkness, combined with an extremely keen sense of smell, makes it a formidable hunter in its deep-sea environment.

These sharks are also known to scavenge, feeding on the carcasses of whales and seals. The shark's large size and powerful jaws allow it to take advantage of these larger food sources, making it a crucial part of the marine ecosystem.

Intriguingly, scientists have found remains of terrestrial animals, such as reindeer and even polar bears, in the stomachs of Greenland Sharks, suggesting that these creatures might feed on carrion that falls into the water or scavenge from the carcasses of animals that have drowned.

Reproduction: A Slow Process

Much like their growth, the reproduction of Greenland Sharks is a slow process. Female sharks are thought to reach sexual maturity at around 150 years of age. They give birth to live young, a process known as viviparity, although the details of their reproductive cycle remain largely unknown due to the difficulty of studying these elusive creatures.

Human Interactions and Threats: A Strained Relationship

Historically, Greenland Sharks were hunted by the Inuit people for their liver oil, which was used as a fuel in lamps. More recently, they have been targeted in commercial fisheries for their flesh, which, after a specific fermentation process, is used to produce a traditional Icelandic dish called Hákarl.

Despite their slow reproduction rate, Greenland Sharks have not been assessed as threatened or endangered, primarily due to their wide distribution and the depth at which they live. However, the impact of fishing, climate change, and ocean pollution on their populations is not well-understood, necessitating further research and potential conservation measures.

Conservation Efforts: Towards a Greater Understanding

Due to the Greenland Shark's elusive nature and the challenging environment in which it lives, scientific understanding of this species is limited. However, recent advancements in technology, such as satellite tagging and genetic analysis, are providing new avenues for research. These studies are critical for assessing the status of Greenland Shark populations and informing conservation strategies.

In recent years, Iceland has led several initiatives focused on the study and conservation of Greenland Sharks. Researchers from the University of Iceland, for example, have been tagging and tracking Greenland Sharks to better understand their migration patterns and behavior. This research will contribute to the broader understanding of this species, and help determine how it may be affected by human activities and climate change.

Another critical aspect of Greenland Shark conservation is public education. Many Icelanders and visitors alike are unaware of the existence of these remarkable sharks in the surrounding waters. Public education campaigns aimed at raising awareness about the Greenland Shark can help foster appreciation for this species and encourage support for its conservation.

Closing Thoughts: Respecting the Denizens of the Deep

The Greenland Shark is a testament to the extraordinary diversity and resilience of life on Earth. These ancient denizens of the deep have roamed the world's oceans for hundreds of years, largely unseen by human eyes. Their slow-paced lifestyle, adapted to the harsh conditions of the Arctic, stands as a stark contrast to the fast-paced change that characterizes the modern world.

As we continue to explore and understand the lives of these remarkable creatures, we must also recognize our responsibility towards their survival. This includes not only direct conservation efforts but also broader actions to protect the health of our oceans. The fate of the Greenland Shark is intrinsically linked with the wellbeing of the marine environment.

The Snow Bunting: Icy Island's Little Songbird

As we delve further into the remarkable wildlife of Iceland, we now turn our attention to one of the country's smallest, yet most captivating residents: the Snow Bunting (Plectrophenax nivalis). Known for its beautiful song and distinctive plumage, this small passerine bird is a treasured part of Iceland's diverse fauna. This chapter will explore the intriguing biology, behavior, and adaptations of the Snow Bunting, and the role it plays in the broader ecological tapestry of Iceland.

Introduction: An Overview of the Snow Bunting

The Snow Bunting, sometimes referred to as the "Snowflake", is a bird of the high Arctic. Despite its small size – typically no more than 15-18 cm in length – this bird is renowned for its resilience and adaptability in the face of harsh Arctic conditions. With a plumage that varies dramatically between the stark white of winter and the brown-spotted coat of summer, the Snow Bunting is a visual testament to the changing seasons.

Adaptations: Surviving the Arctic Chill

Surviving in the harsh Arctic environment requires a suite of specialized adaptations, and the Snow Bunting is no exception. Its thick plumage offers insulation against the freezing temperatures, while its strong, pointed beak allows it to forage effectively in the snow for seeds and insects.

Interestingly, the Snow Bunting is also one of the few passerine species capable of undergoing a complete molt twice a year. This allows the bird to change its plumage to suit the season – a snowy white for winter to blend with the snow-covered landscape and a brown, spotty coat for the summer to provide camouflage among the rocks and vegetation.

Behavior and Lifecycle: A Year in the Life of a Snow Bunting

Snow Buntings are migratory birds. While they breed in the Arctic regions, including the highlands of Iceland, they spend their winters further south, in parts of mainland Europe, Asia, and North America. The onset of the breeding season in late May sees the male Snow Buntings arrive first, staking out territories and preparing nests to attract females.

The female Snow Bunting lays a clutch of 3-7 eggs, which she incubates for about two weeks. During this time, the male guards the territory and brings food to the female. After the chicks hatch, both parents share the responsibility of feeding and caring for them until they fledge, typically around two weeks later.

One of the most captivating aspects of the Snow Bunting is its beautiful song. Male Snow Buntings are known for their melodic, warbling song, which they use to attract mates and defend their territories. These songs, often delivered from a high, exposed perch or during a fluttering flight, are a defining sound of the Arctic summer.

Threats and Conservation: Protecting the Snow Buntings

Like many Arctic species, the Snow Bunting faces a range of threats, primarily linked to climate change and habitat loss.

Changes in temperature and weather patterns can affect the availability of food and nesting sites, while human activities, such as farming and development, can lead to habitat loss.

Despite these threats, the Snow Bunting is currently listed as of Least Concern by the International Union for Conservation of Nature (IUCN). However, ongoing monitoring is necessary to track potential changes in population trends and respond to any emerging threats.

The Song of the Arctic

The Snow Bunting is more than just a bird – it's a symbol of the Arctic, embodying the resilience and beauty of this harsh yet awe-inspiring region. As we learn more about these charming songbirds, we are reminded of the intricate web of life that characterizes the Icelandic landscape.

For the people of Iceland, the annual arrival of the Snow Bunting signifies the onset of spring. Their melodious songs fill the air, adding a unique soundtrack to the stunning Icelandic landscape. Observing these birds, one can't help but marvel at their tenacity and the intricate balance of nature that allows such small creatures to thrive in such a challenging environment.

Understanding the Snow Bunting's Migration Patterns

One of the most intriguing aspects of the Snow Bunting's lifecycle is its migration. The journey these birds undertake each year is a testament to their endurance and navigational prowess. Each spring, they travel from their wintering grounds in the temperate regions to the high Arctic, a journey of thousands of kilometers.

Scientists are still unraveling the mysteries of how they navigate these vast distances. Current research suggests a combination of celestial cues, the Earth's magnetic field, and perhaps even olfactory landmarks may guide them on their journey. As technology and research methods continue to advance, we will undoubtedly gain deeper insight into this remarkable feat.

The Ecological Role of the Snow Bunting

While small in stature, the Snow Bunting plays a significant role in its ecosystem. Through its feeding habits, it helps control insect populations during the summer months. Meanwhile, its predation on seeds aids in the dispersal of several plant species, contributing to the biodiversity of the regions it inhabits.

In turn, the Snow Bunting forms a vital link in the food chain, serving as prey for larger birds of prey like gyrfalcons and Arctic foxes. Thus, the wellbeing of the Snow Bunting population can often reflect the overall health of the ecosystem.

The Cultural Significance of the Snow Bunting in Iceland

In Iceland, the Snow Bunting holds a special place in local culture. Its arrival is eagerly awaited each spring, signaling the end of the long, harsh winter. The bird's beautiful song and striking plumage have made it a beloved symbol of the Icelandic wilderness, and it features prominently in local folklore and literature.

For instance, there's an old Icelandic saying, "When the Snow Bunting arrives, spring is here," reflecting the bird's close association with the changing seasons. Similarly, Icelandic poetry and music often reference the Snow Bunting, further highlighting its cultural significance.

The Atlantic Salmon's Epic Journey

Atlantic Salmon, known by the scientific name Salmo salar, meaning "leaping salmon," is a species of ray-finned fish in the family Salmonidae. It is found in the northern Atlantic Ocean and in rivers that flow into the North Atlantic. The Atlantic Salmon's remarkable lifecycle, involving a dramatic migration from freshwater streams to the ocean and back again, has fascinated scientists and nature enthusiasts alike, warranting a deep exploration of this splendid species.

Life Begins in Freshwater: The Early Stages

Atlantic Salmon begin their lives in the cold, clear waters of freshwater rivers and streams. Female salmon, known as 'hens,' create nests called 'redds' in the riverbed, where they lay their eggs. The male salmon then fertilize these eggs, and the resulting embryos develop over the winter, hatching into tiny larvae called 'alevins' in the spring.

These alevins remain in the relative safety of the gravel riverbed, living off a yolk sac attached to their bodies. As the yolk sac depletes, the alevins emerge from the gravel and start to feed on small insects, taking on the name 'fry.' As they grow, they develop distinctive markings known as 'parr marks' and are thus called 'parr.'

The Journey to Sea: Smoltification

After one to six years in freshwater, depending on their growth rate and the productivity of their home stream, the parr undergo a fascinating metamorphosis known as 'smoltification.' During this process, their bodies adapt to living in saltwater. Their color changes from a camouflaged brown to a silvery blue, better suited to the open ocean, and their physiological systems undergo dramatic changes to enable them to survive in a marine environment.

The oceanic journey begins in the spring when these 'smolts' are carried downstream to the estuary, where the river meets the sea. Here, they spend some time acclimating to the saltwater before venturing out into the open ocean.

Life in the Ocean: The Feeding Phase

In the marine environment, Atlantic Salmon grow rapidly, feeding on a diet of shrimp, squid, and fish. They can spend one to four years in the ocean, journeying thousands of kilometers from their home rivers. Their migration routes are still somewhat of a mystery to scientists, but they are thought to travel to the nutrient-rich waters of Greenland and the Faroe Islands.

The Return Home: Spawning Migration

Perhaps the most astonishing part of the Atlantic Salmon's lifecycle is their ability to return to the exact river where they were born to spawn. This impressive navigational feat is still not fully understood, but it is believed to involve a combination of sensing the Earth's magnetic field and olfactory cues.

These mature salmon, known as 'grilse,' cease feeding upon entering freshwater and must navigate countless obstacles, including waterfalls and rapids, to reach their spawning grounds. Their journey is fraught with peril, as they face threats from predators, human-made barriers, and pollution.

The End and the Beginning: Spawning and Mortality

Once they reach their natal streams, the females dig redds and lay their eggs, and the cycle of life begins anew. It's important to note that unlike Pacific Salmon, Atlantic Salmon do not necessarily die after spawning; some manage to return to the sea and may repeat the migration and spawning process.

The Atlantic Salmon, a Symbol of Endurance and Adaptation

The Atlantic Salmon's epic journey, from the freshwater streams to the vast ocean and back, is a testament to the wonders of natural adaptation and endurance. Their complex lifecycle, spanning freshwater and marine environments, makes them a critical link between these ecosystems.

However, Atlantic Salmon populations have been in decline in recent years due to a combination of factors including overfishing, habitat destruction, pollution, and climate change. This decline is a matter of grave concern as the loss of this species could significantly disrupt the ecological balance of both freshwater and marine environments.

The Icelandic rivers, such as the Ranga and the Laxa in Adaldal, are known as some of the most bountiful salmon rivers in the world. As such, they are a critical habitat for the Atlantic Salmon and play a crucial role in the survival of this species. These rivers offer relatively pristine environments for the salmon to breed and grow, making Iceland an important stakeholder in the conservation of Atlantic Salmon.

Conservation efforts for the Atlantic Salmon in Iceland and elsewhere are multifaceted, focusing on reducing overfishing, restoring and protecting critical habitats, and monitoring populations to collect data for research and management purposes. These efforts are crucial to ensuring that future generations can continue to marvel at the epic journey of the Atlantic Salmon and to benefit from the ecological services they provide.

In conclusion, the Atlantic Salmon is a remarkable creature that epitomizes the relentless drive for survival that characterizes life on Earth. Its epic journey from the rivers of Iceland to the North Atlantic and back is a marvel of the natural world and a story of adaptation, endurance, and the interconnectedness of life. Through understanding and appreciating these wonders of nature, we can better recognize the importance of protecting and preserving them for the generations to come. The Atlantic Salmon's journey is not just a fish's tale; it's a testament to the incredible tapestry of life that our planet supports, and of our responsibility to preserve it.

Short-eared Owls: Hunters of the Midnight Sun

As the sun hangs low on the horizon, refusing to set beneath the veil of the endless summer twilight, the quiet of the Icelandic wilderness is broken by a soft, haunting hoot. Silhouetted against the backdrop of the midnight sun, the Short-eared Owl (Asio flammeus) emerges as one of the most fascinating avian denizens of this northern paradise.

Short-eared Owls are among the most widespread owl species, found on every continent except Australia and Antarctica. Yet, in the unique environmental context of Iceland, they take on an added level of intrigue. Their name derives from the small, feathered tufts on their heads, which resemble ears. However, these "ears" are not always visible and play no role in the owl's exceptional hearing, which is actually facilitated by their asymmetrical ear openings.

An enigma of the Icelandic skies, the Short-eared Owl is one of the few raptors that are primarily diurnal, meaning they are active during the day. However, in the land of the midnight sun, these owls adjust their hunting patterns to match the extended daylight hours of the Icelandic summer, becoming crepuscular and even nocturnal hunters.

Short-eared Owls primarily prey upon small mammals, with voles being their preferred meal. However, they are opportunistic hunters and will also take birds if the opportunity presents itself. Their hunting strategy is a sight to behold. They glide low over open fields and marshlands, using their acute sense of hearing to detect the movements of hidden prey. Upon locating a potential meal, they will hover momentarily before diving talons-first into the grass.

Their breeding habits are equally fascinating. Rather than maintaining a permanent nesting site, Short-eared Owls are nomadic breeders, moving their nesting locations based on the availability of prey. This nomadic lifestyle is facilitated by their ground-nesting behavior. The female will create a shallow depression in the ground, typically in a well-hidden location amidst tall grass or heather.

The relationship between Short-eared Owls and the Icelandic environment is a testament to the interconnectedness of ecosystems. Changes in vole populations can directly influence the distribution, reproductive success, and population density of these owls. Thus, monitoring the Short-eared Owl can provide valuable insights into the overall health of the ecosystem.

Yet, this reliance on fluctuating prey populations also makes Short-eared Owls vulnerable. Habitat destruction and the use of rodenticides can significantly impact their survival. Hence, conservation efforts aimed at preserving the pristine wilderness of Iceland have a direct bearing on the future of these enchanting owls.

The Short-eared Owl is a captivating subject of study and observation, embodying the wild, untamed spirit of Iceland's natural world. They remind us of the intricate tapestry of life that thrives in this stark, beautiful landscape, where the glow of the midnight sun illuminates a world teeming with wonder and mystery.

The Atlantic Puffin's Close Relative: The Razorbill

In the diverse avian world of Iceland, one bird stands out as the Atlantic Puffin's closest relative — the Razorbill (Alca torda). Sharing the same family, Alcidae, the Razorbill is a captivating species with its own unique characteristics and behaviors that add depth and intrigue to the complex tapestry of Iceland's birdlife.

The Razorbill, with its sleek black-and-white plumage and a large, sharp beak from which it gets its name, is an icon of the North Atlantic's rugged coastal cliffs. They are slightly larger than puffins, measuring around 38-43 cm in length, with a wingspan reaching up to 70 cm. Their black upperparts contrast sharply with their white underparts, creating a striking monochromatic look. The Razorbill's beak, thick and black, is marked by a distinctive white line, adding to their unique appearance.

This bird's life is tied to the sea. They spend most of their lives out on the open ocean, only returning to land during the breeding season. Their powerful wings, which beat swiftly as they fly, also serve as efficient paddles underwater. Razorbills are exceptional divers, capable of reaching depths up to 120 meters in search of fish and crustaceans.

When the breeding season arrives, usually from May to July, Razorbills return to their cliff-side nesting colonies. These colonies are often shared with other seabirds, including their famous relatives, the Atlantic Puffins. The mating pairs, which are monogamous and mate for life, lay a single egg each year. This egg is unique among bird species — it's pear-shaped. The pointed end of the egg helps prevent it from rolling off the cliff ledges, providing an ingenious adaptation to their precarious nesting sites.

Both Razorbill parents share the responsibility of incubating the egg and raising the chick, a testament to their strong pair bonds. After approximately 35 to 37 days of incubation, the chick hatches, entering a world perched high above the crashing waves. The chick, or 'jumpling,' will leave the nest after just 20 days, long before it can fly, making a daring leap into the sea below under the watchful eyes of the male parent, who will continue to care for it at sea.

Despite their robust populations, Razorbills face several threats that could impact their future. Climate change and overfishing are primary concerns, as they alter the delicate balance of the marine ecosystems that these birds rely on. Pollution, particularly oil spills, pose a significant threat, damaging their waterproof plumage and contaminating their food sources. It's a reminder of our shared responsibility to protect these incredible creatures and the wild, untamed landscapes they inhabit.

The Razorbill's story is one of resilience and adaptation, a narrative written in the heart of the wild North Atlantic. They represent an integral link in the complex web of life that extends from the deepest ocean trenches to the highest clifftop rookeries. In their striking black and white attire, they encapsulate the raw, captivating beauty of Iceland's rich biodiversity.

The Red-throated Loon: An Arctic Coastal Gem

In the chill of the Arctic, among the seemingly barren coastal landscapes, one bird showcases an extraordinary spectacle of nature — the Red-throated Loon (Gavia stellata). This captivating avian species, marked by its vibrant throat patch and intricate feather patterns, is a treasure of Iceland's coastal ecology and a symbol of the harsh yet wondrous Arctic environment.

The Red-throated Loon, also known as the Red-throated Diver in some regions, is the smallest and most widely distributed member of the loon family. Measuring approximately 55-67 cm in length with a wingspan of about 105-115 cm, it carries a distinctive profile. In its summer plumage, this loon exhibits a grayish-blue head, a patterned back with intricate checkered spotting, and most notably, a triangular patch of brilliant reddish-pink on its throat, lending the bird its common name.

Unlike its larger loon relatives, the Red-throated Loon's legs are positioned slightly more forward, allowing it to move on land with more agility — a useful adaptation for a bird that nests on tundra lakes and ponds, often quite some distance from the sea.

The marine realm is where this species truly excels, with its streamlined body and powerful, webbed feet propelling it through water in pursuit of fish, its primary diet. Capable of diving to depths of up to 30 meters, the Red-throated Loon is a formidable hunter, demonstrating extraordinary underwater agility as it chases down prey.

Breeding from May to August, the Red-throated Loon exhibits monogamous behavior, with pair bonds often lasting for life. They build their nests close to the water's edge, usually a simple scrape in the ground lined with vegetation. In this intimate setting, both parents share the responsibility of incubating the one or two eggs, which hatch after about 24-29 days.

The chicks are precocial, meaning they are relatively mature and mobile from the moment of hatching. Even so, the parents continue to nurture and protect them, often carrying the chicks on their backs while swimming during their first few weeks of life. The chicks are able to fly and become independent after about 6-7 weeks, embarking on their own journey within the vast Arctic landscape.

The hauntingly beautiful call of the Red-throated Loon, a series of wailing and yodeling notes, is emblematic of the Arctic wilderness and has featured in folklore and literature of the northern cultures.

However, the Red-throated Loon is not immune to the threats that face many of the world's bird species today. Climate change, habitat loss, and pollution, particularly by plastic waste and lead fishing tackle, are significant concerns for this Arctic species. As such, their status serves as an important indicator of the health of the Arctic and subarctic ecosystems.

In the panoramic landscapes of Iceland, the Red-throated Loon stands as a beacon of the Arctic's enduring charm. Its presence reminds us of the delicate balance that exists in nature and our role in preserving these environments. The life of the Red-throated Loon, vibrant yet vulnerable, is a testament to the marvels of the natural world and the intricate web of life that binds us all.

The Enigmatic Harbor Porpoise

In the rich, teeming waters surrounding Iceland, one creature personifies the enigmatic charm of marine life - the Harbor Porpoise (Phocoena phocoena). These small, shy, and elusive cetaceans are a captivating sight, revealing the intricate harmony that exists beneath the surface of the North Atlantic and Arctic Oceans.

The Harbor Porpoise is one of the smallest marine mammals, typically measuring between 1.4 to 1.9 meters in length and weighing around 45 to 60 kilograms. Their bodies are robust and streamlined, designed for a life of swift and efficient movement through their aquatic domain. Their skin exhibits a counter-shaded color pattern - a dark grey back and lighter grey sides and belly, which provides them with effective camouflage against both predators and prey.

One of the distinguishing features of the Harbor Porpoise is its small, triangular dorsal fin located midway down its back.

Unlike their dolphin relatives, porpoises have a blunt, rounded snout and spade-shaped teeth, characteristics that can be used to distinguish them in the rare event of a close encounter.

These elusive creatures are typically solitary or found in small groups. They are known for their quiet demeanor, surfacing gently with a characteristic rolling motion, often without showing their dorsal fin, and disappearing as quickly and quietly as they appeared.

Harbor Porpoises are widely distributed and can be found in coastal waters, bays, estuaries, and occasionally in rivers. In the waters around Iceland, they are most commonly sighted during the summer months. They feed on a variety of fish species, as well as squid and crustaceans, consuming up to 10% of their body weight each day to support their high metabolic rate.

Their life cycle is relatively short compared to other cetaceans. Females reach sexual maturity at around 3-4 years, while males mature slightly later. After a gestation period of about 10-11 months, females give birth to a single calf. The bond between mother and calf is strong, with the calf dependent on its mother's rich milk for up to 9 months.

The Harbor Porpoise, despite its widespread distribution, is facing increasing threats. Incidental catch (bycatch) in fishing gear is one of the leading causes of mortality for this species. Pollution, habitat degradation, and disturbances from vessel traffic are additional factors that contribute to their vulnerability.

Despite their elusive nature, Harbor Porpoises have a role in human culture. In Norse mythology, they were considered sacred to the god Freyr, who was associated with prosperity and good harvest. Today, their presence and health are considered important indicators of the overall health of the marine ecosystem.

In conclusion, the Harbor Porpoise, with its delicate presence and elusive behavior, encapsulates the mystery and allure of Iceland's marine environment. Their silent surfacing and swift disappearance serve as a reminder of the hidden wonders beneath the waves, the intricate web of life that thrives beneath the surface, and our responsibility to protect and preserve these unique creatures and their habitat.

Kittiwakes: The Cliffside Nesters

There is a unique charm to the cliffs of Iceland during the summer months. Amidst the dramatic landscape, you'll hear the echoing calls of Kittiwakes, the cliffside nesters. Belonging to the gull family, the Kittiwake (Rissa tridactyla) is a beloved part of Iceland's avian community, easily identifiable by their distinctive 'kitti-wake' calls, from which they earn their common name.

Kittiwakes are smaller than the typical gull, measuring about 37-41 centimeters in length with a wingspan of around a meter. They exhibit a graceful flight pattern, their slender wings allowing them to hover and swoop with elegance. Their plumage is a simple, elegant contrast of white and grey: a white body, light grey wings, and darker grey wingtips, their black legs and yellow bill complementing this understated palette.

The life of a Kittiwake revolves around the sea and the cliffs. They spend most of the year in the open ocean, feeding primarily on small fish and invertebrates like shrimp and squid. Their keen eyes and agile flight make them effective hunters, capable of spotting and diving for prey from considerable heights.

But it is during the breeding season, from April to August, that the Kittiwakes truly come to life. They return to their nesting sites, favoring the steep sea cliffs of Iceland's coastlines, forming large colonies that can number in the thousands. A Kittiwake colony in the breeding season is a spectacle to behold, a cacophony of calls and a flurry of white and grey against the stark cliff faces.

Kittiwakes are monogamous and display exceptional nest fidelity, often returning to the exact same nesting spot year after year. They build their nests on narrow cliff ledges, using seaweed, grass, and mud, the structure glued together with their droppings. Both parents share the responsibility of incubating the eggs, which are usually two in number, and raising the chicks.

The Kittiwake chicks, or 'kittlins', are born semi-precocial, covered in down and with their eyes open. They stay in the nest for about six weeks, during which time they are fed and cared for by both parents. By the end of the summer, the fledglings are ready to take their first flight, marking the end of the breeding season.

In recent years, the Kittiwake population in some parts of the world has seen a significant decline, largely due to factors such as overfishing and climate change affecting their food supply. However, in Iceland, their numbers remain relatively stable, partly due to stringent fishing regulations and the availability of suitable nesting sites.

Despite these challenges, Kittiwakes continue to captivate birdwatchers and nature lovers with their beauty and resilience. Their presence is a symbol of the wild, untamed spirit of the Icelandic coasts. As the summer sun sets, painting the sky with hues of orange and purple, the silhouette of a Kittiwake soaring above the ocean waves is a sight that encapsulates the awe-inspiring beauty of Iceland's animal kingdom.

In summary, the Kittiwake's story is one of endurance and adaptability. These cliffside nesters are a testament to the resilience of life amidst the harsh conditions of the North Atlantic. Their melodious calls, echoing against the cliffs of Iceland, are a reminder of the intricate balance of nature and our responsibility to preserve it for future generations.

The Black Guillemot: A Contrast in Plumage

In the world of Icelandic birds, the Black Guillemot (Cepphus grylle) stands out for its striking contrast in plumage. Also known as the Tystie, this charming seabird is a testament to the beauty of nature's palette, a splash of monochrome against the azure blues of the North Atlantic.

The Black Guillemot is a medium-sized bird, typically measuring about 30-38 centimeters in length with a wingspan ranging from 49 to 58 centimeters. It has a distinctive plumage that undergoes a fascinating transformation across seasons. In the summer breeding season, the adult Black Guillemot boasts a sleek, all-black body, complemented by white wing patches that are visible in flight. This monochrome look is paired with bright red feet and a thin, black bill, making it an unmistakable sight.

However, come winter, the Black Guillemot undergoes a transformation. It trades its dark summer feathers for a predominantly white plumage, with only the wings retaining a scaled black and white pattern. This seasonal wardrobe change aids in camouflage, blending with the snowy winter landscapes and icy waters.

The Black Guillemot is a marine bird, spending the majority of its life at sea. Their diet primarily consists of fish, supplemented with crustaceans and other small marine creatures. They're adept divers, using their wings to propel themselves underwater in pursuit of their prey.

Breeding season, typically from May to August, brings Black Guillemots closer to land. They favor rocky shores and cliffs for nesting, often choosing crevices or holes in which to lay their eggs. An interesting aspect of Black Guillemot behavior is their adaptability when it comes to nesting sites. They've been known to use a variety of locations, from natural rock formations to man-made structures like piers and even rooftops.

Black Guillemots lay one to two eggs, and both parents share the responsibility of incubation, which lasts for about a month. After the chicks hatch, both parents also take turns feeding the young, primarily with fish. By late summer, the chicks are ready to fledge and embark on their journey into the wide ocean.

Though not as numerous as some of their puffin or gull counterparts, Black Guillemots form a vital part of the marine ecosystem around Iceland. Their population trends are often considered indicators of the health of the marine environment, as changes can reflect shifts in fish populations and overall oceanic conditions.

Despite facing challenges from factors like climate change and marine pollution, Black Guillemots continue to thrive in the harsh conditions of the North Atlantic, thanks in part to their adaptability and resilience. Their striking seasonal plumage and fascinating behavior make them a favorite among birdwatchers and nature enthusiasts, a feathered symbol of Iceland's rich biodiversity.

In conclusion, the Black Guillemot, with its striking contrast in plumage and captivating life cycle, is a beautiful embodiment of Iceland's wildlife. Its story is a testament to nature's adaptability and resilience, an inspiring narrative that unfolds on the rocky cliffs and in the icy waters of the North Atlantic. The Black Guillemot serves as a reminder of the wonders that lie in the wild, untouched corners of our world and the importance of preserving them for future generations.

The Redwing: An Icelandic Songbird Saga

Every nation has its emblematic wildlife that carries a unique story, intertwined with its cultural and natural landscapes. For Iceland, the Redwing (Turdus iliacus) is one such creature - a songbird that weaves an enchanting saga throughout the year.

The Redwing is a member of the thrush family, which includes other renowned songbirds like the American Robin and the European Blackbird. Smaller than many of its relatives, the Redwing measures about 20-24 cm in length. Its name is a tribute to its most distinguishing feature - the rusty-red flanks and underwing feathers that contrast with its otherwise brownish upperparts and streaked underparts. The Redwing's striking appearance is completed with a distinct whitish eyebrow stripe, adding a dash of flair to its overall plumage.

Redwings are primarily insectivorous during the summer months, hunting for invertebrates in the undergrowth and soil. As the colder months approach and the availability of insects dwindles, they switch their diet to berries and fruits, showcasing a commendable adaptability in their feeding habits.

In Iceland, the Redwing holds the unique distinction of being the only thrush species that breeds on the island. Their breeding season typically starts in May and extends till July. They prefer to nest in shrubs, low trees, or on the ground, tucked away amidst tall vegetation. Each clutch usually consists of 4-6 eggs, which are pale blue with blackish spots, and incubation is primarily the female's duty.

One of the most captivating aspects of the Redwing's existence is its melodic song. A complex cascade of notes, trills, and whistles, the Redwing's song is among the most beautiful in the avian world. It is during the breeding season that their music is most prevalent, filling the Icelandic landscapes with a harmonious symphony that announces the arrival of spring.

The saga of the Redwing takes a dramatic turn with the onset of winter. As temperatures plummet, most Redwings migrate south, journeying to the British Isles and mainland Europe, where conditions are milder. However, some choose to brave the harsh Icelandic winter, making them a year-round fixture of the country's avifauna.

The Redwing is not only significant in the context of Iceland's biodiversity but also holds cultural importance. Its melodious song is a symbol of the advent of spring, and its presence or absence is often seen as a marker of the changing seasons. Moreover, the Redwing is also the national bird of Iceland, further cementing its status in the country's cultural and natural identity.

In conclusion, the saga of the Redwing is a captivating narrative that transcends the realms of ecology and enters folklore and symbolism. This unassuming yet enchanting songbird, with its beautiful plumage and melodious song, is a living testament to Iceland's rich natural heritage. The Redwing's story, resounding with themes of adaptability, survival, and beauty, continues to unfold with each passing season, adding new chapters to an already fascinating Icelandic songbird saga.

Seabird Spectacle: The Arctic Tern

For many, the term "long-distance traveler" might evoke images of migratory mammals like the humpback whale or the caribou. Yet, in the world of avian migrations, one seabird stands unchallenged: the Arctic Tern (Sterna paradisaea). This small, elegant bird, with its extraordinary migratory journey, provides one of nature's most spectacular performances.

The Arctic Tern is a graceful and slender bird, reaching a length of approximately 33-39 cm. It sports a predominantly light grey and white plumage, with a distinguishing black cap covering its head during the breeding season. Its deeply forked tail, long wings, and red beak and feet further add to its distinctive appearance.

As the name suggests, the Arctic Tern is a creature of the polar regions, breeding in the Arctic during the northern summer. Its nesting grounds are typically open areas near water bodies, such as coastlines, islands, and marshes. The tern's nests are simple scrapes on the ground, often lined with vegetation or small stones. The female typically lays one to three eggs, and both parents share the duties of incubation and feeding the chicks.

Yet, the Arctic Tern is not just an Arctic bird. As the northern summer draws to a close, these birds embark on a phenomenal migratory journey to the other end of the world, the Antarctic. This round-trip voyage covers a staggering 70,000 kilometers each year, the longest-known migration in the animal kingdom. During this journey, the Arctic Tern experiences more daylight than any other creature on Earth, earning it the title of the 'bird of the midnight sun'.

The primary diet of the Arctic Tern consists of small fish and invertebrates, which it catches by executing swift, elegant dives into the water from flight. These terns are also known for their aggressive nature when defending their nests, often attacking much larger predators that venture too close.

One of the most captivating aspects of observing Arctic Terns in Iceland is their acrobatic flight displays during courtship and territorial disputes. These aerial performances involve high-speed chases, spiraling ascents, and sudden nose-dives, showcasing their exceptional flight capabilities.

The Arctic Tern holds a significant role in the Icelandic cultural and natural landscapes. Its annual arrival in May signals the onset of summer and its departure in late August or early September heralds the approaching winter. The return of the terns from their Antarctic sojourn is eagerly awaited each year and is celebrated with festivals in some parts of Iceland.

In the broader context of conservation, the Arctic Tern serves as an indicator species for the health of marine ecosystems. Changes in their numbers or behavior can reflect alterations in food availability and climate conditions, providing vital cues for environmental monitoring.

In conclusion, the Arctic Tern, with its awe-inspiring migration, elegant flight, and integral role in seasonal transitions, is a true spectacle of the seabird world. Whether it's soaring against the backdrop of an Icelandic summer sky or navigating the vast expanses of the world's oceans, the Arctic Tern's story is one of resilience, endurance, and breathtaking natural beauty. It serves as a vivid reminder of the intricate and extraordinary journeys that define our planet's wildlife.

The Unassuming Meadow Pipit

In the vast landscapes of Iceland, where the grandeur of glaciers, volcanoes, and waterfalls often steal the show, it's easy to overlook the smaller, less flamboyant inhabitants of this island nation. One such creature is the Meadow Pipit (Anthus pratensis), a modest bird that might lack the ostentatious colors of some of its avian counterparts but boasts a charm that is all its own.

The Meadow Pipit is a small passerine bird, about 14-15 cm long, belonging to the family Motacillidae, which also includes wagtails and longclaws. It has a generally brownish, streaked plumage that blends well with its preferred habitats, making it somewhat challenging to spot. Its belly is paler with distinctive dark streaking, and it has a thin beak perfectly adapted for its insectivorous diet.

One of the Meadow Pipit's most distinguishing characteristics is its flight pattern. When taking off, these birds display a characteristic series of rapid wingbeats followed by a short glide, creating an undulating flight pattern that is often the first clue to their presence in a field or meadow.

While they may be unassuming in appearance, Meadow Pipits come into their own through their song. During the breeding season, males perform a 'song flight,' where they rise steeply into the air and then slowly descend while singing a beautiful, high-pitched melody. This display, often performed from dawn to dusk, is one of the sounds that define the Icelandic summer.

Meadow Pipits are ground nesters, typically building their nests in dense vegetation. The female constructs the nest, which is a simple cup-shaped structure made of grass and lined with finer materials. She lays and incubates four to six speckled eggs, and once hatched, both parents share the duties of feeding the chicks.

A significant aspect of the Meadow Pipit's life in Iceland is its relationship with the parasitic Common Cuckoo. In a fascinating and somewhat unsettling display of nature's complexity, the cuckoo lays its eggs in the nests of unsuspecting pipits. The cuckoo chick, once hatched, typically ejects the pipit's eggs or chicks from the nest, ensuring it gets the undivided attention of its foster parents.

The Meadow Pipit's diet consists mainly of invertebrates, such as beetles, spiders, and larvae. During the winter months, when invertebrates are less abundant, they supplement their diet with seeds.

Despite their modesty, Meadow Pipits play a vital role in the ecosystem. They are an essential part of the food chain, serving as prey for larger birds and helping control insect populations. They are also significant indicators of the health of the meadow ecosystems they inhabit, with their population trends reflecting changes in these habitats.

In conclusion, the Meadow Pipit, though often overlooked, is a bird that embodies the quieter, less dramatic aspects of nature that are as important to an ecosystem's harmony as the more spectacular ones. These small birds, with their wavering flight and melodious song, add another layer to the rich tapestry of Icelandic wildlife. They remind us that every creature, no matter how unassuming, has its unique role and charm in the grand scheme of nature.

Eider Ducks: Guardians of the Down

The Common Eider (Somateria mollissima) is a large sea duck that graces the coastal waters of the North Atlantic. Renowned for its luxurious down, the eider holds a unique place in the hearts of Icelanders and the annals of Icelandic wildlife.

The adult male eider is a striking bird, with a black and white body, pale green nape, and a prominent wedge-shaped head. Its beak, long and sloping, is designed for its primary diet of mussels, crustaceans, and other marine invertebrates. The female eider, on the other hand, boasts a more subdued coloration, with a mottled brown plumage that provides excellent camouflage while nesting.

Eiders are gregarious birds, often seen in large flocks on the sea or along the coast. They are powerful swimmers, capable of diving to considerable depths to forage on the seafloor. Their flight, although swift, is labored, requiring a considerable run-up along the water's surface before becoming airborne.

The eider's life cycle revolves around coastal habitats. They nest in colonies, often returning to the same location year after year. The nesting period, which occurs from late May to early June, is a time when the eider's unique relationship with humans is most apparent in Iceland.

Eider down, the soft under-feathers of the female eider, is a commodity treasured worldwide for its insulating properties. Unlike other birds, the eider willingly gives up its down. The female plucks the down from her own breast to line her nest, creating a warm and safe haven for her eggs. Icelandic farmers protect and watch over these nesting colonies, providing safety from predators. In return, they collect the down once the nesting season is over, ensuring the process does not disturb the birds.

The eider's nest is a simple structure, usually located in vegetation or among rocks. The female lays four to five eggs and remains on the nest to incubate them. During this period, she does not eat, relying on body reserves for sustenance.

Once hatched, eider ducklings are precocial - they are well-developed and can leave the nest within a day. The mother leads her brood to the water, where they immediately start to feed themselves. However, they remain under the protective watch of their mother until they fledge, usually in late July or early August.

The eider's diet consists predominantly of shellfish. Using their specialized beaks, they can dive to the bottom and dislodge mussels and other shellfish from the substrate. Back on the surface, they swallow their catch whole, crushing the shells in their muscular gizzard to digest the nutritious animal inside.

The Common Eider is not just an iconic Icelandic bird but a symbol of the potential for harmonious and beneficial coexistence between humans and wildlife. The sustainable harvest of eider down has been practiced for centuries and continues to provide a vital income for many coastal communities in Iceland.

In the grand narrative of Iceland's wildlife, the eider duck represents a tale of symbiosis and survival. These hardy birds, braving the chill of the North Atlantic and flourishing, are a testament to the remarkable adaptability of life. The eider duck's story, like the down they so generously provide, adds another layer of warmth and richness to the complex tapestry of Icelandic nature.

The Wandering Whooper Swan

The Whooper Swan (Cygnus cygnus) is an emblem of Icelandic wildlife, gracing both the land and waters of this northern island with its majestic presence. A tale of elegance and endurance, the whooper swan's journey is woven deeply into the fabric of Icelandic natural history.

This large bird, the biggest of all the swan species, is a spectacle to behold. It flaunts a long, sinuous neck, a hefty body, and broad wings that, when fully extended, can span up to 2.7 meters. The whooper swan's plumage is entirely white, providing a stark contrast against Iceland's volcanic landscape, and a beacon of brightness in the winter months. Its black and yellow beak is another defining feature, setting it apart from the mute swans and Bewick's swans, its closest relatives.

The migratory patterns of the whooper swan are as fascinating as the bird itself. Although a portion of the population stays in Iceland year-round, most embark on an epic journey every year. These birds are among the first to arrive in the spring and the last to leave in the fall, making the most of the Icelandic summer.

In spring, the whooper swans return from their wintering grounds in the British Isles and western Europe. Their arrival is celebrated in Icelandic folklore as a harbinger of the coming summer. Once they arrive, they disperse throughout the country, nesting on freshwater lakes and slow-flowing rivers. The nests are large and mound-like, usually constructed in close proximity to water.

The clutch size typically ranges from four to seven eggs, and both parents share in the incubation duties. Once hatched, the cygnets are grey-brown in color, gradually becoming white as they mature. They are tended to by both parents and remain with them throughout the winter migration and return journey, only separating in the second spring.

The diet of the whooper swan is omnivorous and includes aquatic plants, grains, and occasionally small invertebrates. They feed by dipping their heads underwater to reach for plants and by grazing on land, often doing so at night when they are less likely to be disturbed.

Come autumn, the family groups gather in large flocks and commence their migration back to the wintering grounds. This journey, often done in stages, can span over 1,300 kilometers. The swans navigate this vast distance with an innate sense of direction, often returning to the same wintering sites each year.

Despite the long and potentially perilous migration, the whooper swan has a long lifespan, often reaching over 20 years in the wild. This longevity, combined with its strong site fidelity, means that individual swans can become familiar figures in the landscapes they inhabit.

The whooper swan's distinctive call, from which it gets its name, is another unique aspect of its persona. The call is a loud and resonant 'whooping' sound, often heard during flight and in their winter territories. This call carries over long distances, adding a magical soundtrack to the Icelandic wilderness.

In the context of Iceland's wildlife, the whooper swan is a symbol of resilience and beauty. Its annual journey, spanning countries and seasons, mirrors the ebb and flow of life in this part of the world. As we follow the flight of the whooper swan, we are reminded of the interconnectedness of ecosystems and the remarkable journeys undertaken by these avian wanderers. The wandering whooper swan, thus, adds another fascinating chapter to the saga of Icelandic wildlife.

The Golden Plover: A Symbol of Spring

In the grand saga of Icelandic wildlife, the Golden Plover (Pluvialis apricaria) holds a place of affection and significance. A medium-sized wading bird, it has come to symbolize the arrival of spring in Icelandic culture, its return from winter migration eagerly anticipated by locals and naturalists alike.

The Golden Plover is an elegant bird, characterized by its round body, relatively short legs, and a bill neither too long nor too short. In its summer plumage, it lives up to its name with a beautiful mix of black and gold feathers dotting its upper body, creating an impression of a field of golden flowers. The bird's underparts turn black, and a striking white stripe separates these from the golden feathers above. In contrast, the winter plumage is a more subdued mix of grey and white, a transformation that ensures it blends in with its winter surroundings.

Despite its delicate appearance, the Golden Plover is a bird of fortitude. Each year, it undertakes a remarkable journey, migrating from its wintering grounds in Western Europe and North Africa to breed in the far reaches of the Arctic, including Iceland. The arrival of the Golden Plover in spring, usually in April, is a significant event in Iceland. It is celebrated in poetry and song, regarded as a sign that the long, harsh winter has ended and that warmer, brighter days are ahead.

Once in Iceland, the Golden Plover chooses a wide range of habitats for nesting, from lowland farmland to upland moorland. It's not uncommon to spot these birds even in city parks and gardens, making them an accessible delight for birdwatchers. The nest is a simple scrape on the ground, often concealed by vegetation. The female usually lays four eggs, their mottled appearance providing excellent camouflage against the backdrop of the Icelandic landscape.

The Golden Plover's diet is diverse and includes invertebrates such as worms, beetles, and other small creatures. The bird's feeding behavior is characterized by a distinctive 'run-stop-peck' pattern, as it chases down its prey across the landscape.

Golden Plovers are known for their distinctive and melodic song, a series of mournful whistles that echo across their breeding grounds. This call, combined with their striking plumage, makes them a standout presence in the Icelandic spring and summer.

As autumn approaches, the Golden Plovers prepare for their return journey. The juveniles depart first, followed by the adults. Their departure is a poignant moment, marking the onset of the harsh Icelandic winter.

In a country known for its hardy inhabitants and rugged landscapes, the Golden Plover has found its place in the heart of the nation. Its spring arrival and autumn departure are markers of the passing seasons, its song a soundtrack to the

Icelandic spring. Through its resilience and charm, the Golden Plover embodies the spirit of the Icelandic wilderness and continues to inspire generations of nature enthusiasts.

The Golden Plover's journey, like that of many migratory birds, is a testament to the remarkable endurance of these small creatures. As we trace their routes across continents, we gain a deeper understanding of the interconnectedness of ecosystems and the need for their conservation. The story of the Golden Plover, thus, serves not just as a symbol of spring, but also as a reminder of our shared responsibility towards the natural world.

The Lesser Black-backed Gull: The Sea's Ever-Present Scavenger

Among the multitude of seabirds that frequent the coasts of Iceland, the Lesser Black-backed Gull (Larus fuscus) stands out as a symbol of resilience and adaptability. Recognizable by its dark grey to black upperparts — a stark contrast to its white underparts — this gull species is a ubiquitous sight along the coastlines and is considered a marine scavenger par excellence.

The Lesser Black-backed Gull is medium to large in size, with a wingspan that can reach up to 150 cm. In addition to its characteristic plumage, the bird sports a yellow bill with a red spot, and its eyes are a bright yellow, rimmed with a narrow red ring. These features, combined with its pink legs, provide a striking contrast against the backdrop of the sea and sky.

What sets the Lesser Black-backed Gull apart from many other seabirds is its exceptional adaptability. It's not just confined to the sea and coastlines; it has successfully colonized inland areas and can often be seen around towns, cities, and even garbage dumps. This adaptability to different environments is testament to the bird's versatile diet, which ranges from fish, invertebrates, and small birds to food scraps and carrion.

The breeding season for the Lesser Black-backed Gull typically begins in May. Nesting colonies are found on cliffs, in marshes, and increasingly, on rooftops in urban areas. The nest itself is a rudimentary construction of vegetation, lined with softer materials such as feathers. The female usually lays two to four eggs, and both parents share the responsibilities of incubation and feeding the young.

Like many gulls, the Lesser Black-backed Gull is known for its aggressive behavior, especially during the breeding season. Intruders venturing too close to the nest are met with loud calls, and if warnings are unheeded, the gulls are not afraid to dive-bomb perceived threats. This protective nature extends to their feeding habits, where they frequently engage in 'kleptoparasitism', stealing food from other birds.

Despite their somewhat notorious reputation, Lesser Black-backed Gulls play a vital role in their ecosystems. As scavengers, they help keep their habitats clean by consuming carrion and waste. They are also indicators of marine health: changes in their population size or breeding success can signal shifts in fish stocks or the presence of pollutants.

The Lesser Black-backed Gull is also a long-distance migrant. The Icelandic population, along with those from other northern regions, typically spends the winter in the warmer climes of Southern Europe and West Africa. These epic journeys further underscore the bird's adaptability and resilience.

In the end, the story of the Lesser Black-backed Gull is a reflection of the dynamic and ever-changing nature of the marine world. Through its ubiquitous presence, it reminds us of the importance of every species in the ecological web. Despite being considered a common sight, the life of the Lesser Black-backed Gull is anything but ordinary, and it continues to thrive amidst the challenges of the wild, riding the winds of change with an unyielding spirit.

Conclusion

As we draw the curtain on our exploration of Icelandic wildlife, we are left with a profound sense of admiration, wonder, and respect for the many creatures that call this Nordic island home. The wildlife of Iceland, from the smallest of insects to the most imposing of marine mammals, is as diverse and dynamic as the landscapes they inhabit.

The stories woven throughout these chapters are not merely narratives of individual species, but rather they form a tapestry that illustrates the interconnectedness of life. Each species, whether it is the majestic gyrfalcon, the resilient reindeer, or the humble meadow pipit, has a role to play in the intricate web of Icelandic ecology.

What comes to the fore in these narratives is the remarkable resilience and adaptability of these creatures. From the harsh volcanic terrain to the frigid glacial expanses, from the stormy seas to the serene freshwater lakes, the wildlife of Iceland has evolved to thrive in an environment that can be as unpredictable as it is beautiful. They endure, and indeed, flourish amidst the cycle of the seasons, each species following its own rhythmic dance of survival and procreation.

And yet, as we reflect on the strength and resilience of these creatures, we are also reminded of their vulnerability. The Arctic tern's epic migratory journey, the reindeer's struggle for survival in harsh winters, the puffin's dependence on ample fish stocks — these stories underscore the delicate balance of nature and the factors that can tip the scales. Climate change, habitat degradation, pollution, and overfishing are just a few of the challenges that these species face.

It is our hope that this book has not only provided you with a deeper understanding of Icelandic wildlife but also inspired a sense of responsibility. As stewards of this planet, it is incumbent upon us to ensure that these stories of survival, adaptation, and resilience continue to unfold. In preserving the habitats and biodiversity of Iceland, we are safeguarding a natural heritage that is not just Icelandic but also truly global.

Iceland's wildlife, much like its landscapes, captivates the imagination and stirs the spirit. They are an integral part of the island's identity and its allure. From the tiniest insects that flutter amidst the summer blooms to the gargantuan whales that traverse its surrounding seas, every creature contributes to the rich symphony of life that resonates across this island nation.

In the grand theatre of nature, every species has a part to play, every life has a story to tell, and every story adds to our collective understanding and appreciation of the natural world. May the tales of these creatures continue to inspire us, reminding us of the beauty, the resilience, and the fragility of life on Earth. In their survival and prosperity, we see a reflection of our own journey on this shared planet.

As we conclude our journey through the fauna of Iceland, let us remember that these narratives are living, breathing stories. They continue to unfold, shaped by the forces of nature and the actions of mankind. May we tread gently on this Earth, respecting and preserving the many forms of life with which we share it. For in their survival, we find our own. And in their stories, we find fragments of our own humanity.

Thank you for joining us on this exploration of Icelandic wildlife. It is our hope that the knowledge and appreciation you have gained will continue to grow and inspire a lifelong love and respect for the natural world. After all, the stories of these creatures are not just tales of survival; they are a testament to the enduring power of life itself.

Printed in Great Britain
by Amazon